C000254015

BURNHAM TO EVERCREECH JUNCTION

Vic Mitchell and Keith Smith

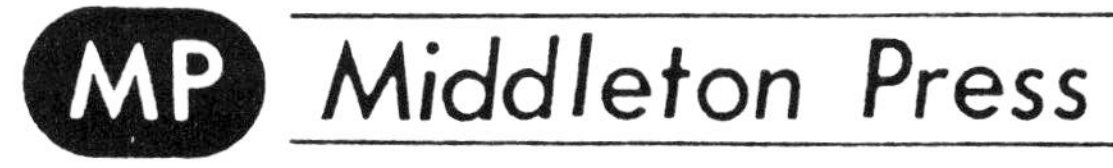

Cover picture: The former Highbridge Works is in the background as passengers amble towards the GWR platforms and LMS 0-6-0 no. 3198 departs for the SDJR terminus at Burnham-on-Sea, on 13th July 1935.
(S. W. Baker)

"Forget motor cars, get rid of anxiety and dream again that ambitious Victorian dream which caused this long railway to be running through deepest, quietest, flattest, remotest, least spoiled Somerset." - Sir John Betjeman in his 1963 TV film *Branch Line Railway*.

First published October 1989

ISBN 0 906520 68 1

Design - Deborah Goodridge

Laser typeset by Barbara Mitchell

Published by Middleton Press
Easebourne Lane
Midhurst, West Sussex
GU29 9AZ
Tel. (0730) 813169

Printed & bound by Biddles Ltd,
Guildford and Kings Lynn

CONTENTS

The SR's first map shows the S & D route as part of their system, with no mention of the joint operation. The GWR is marked with narrower lines.

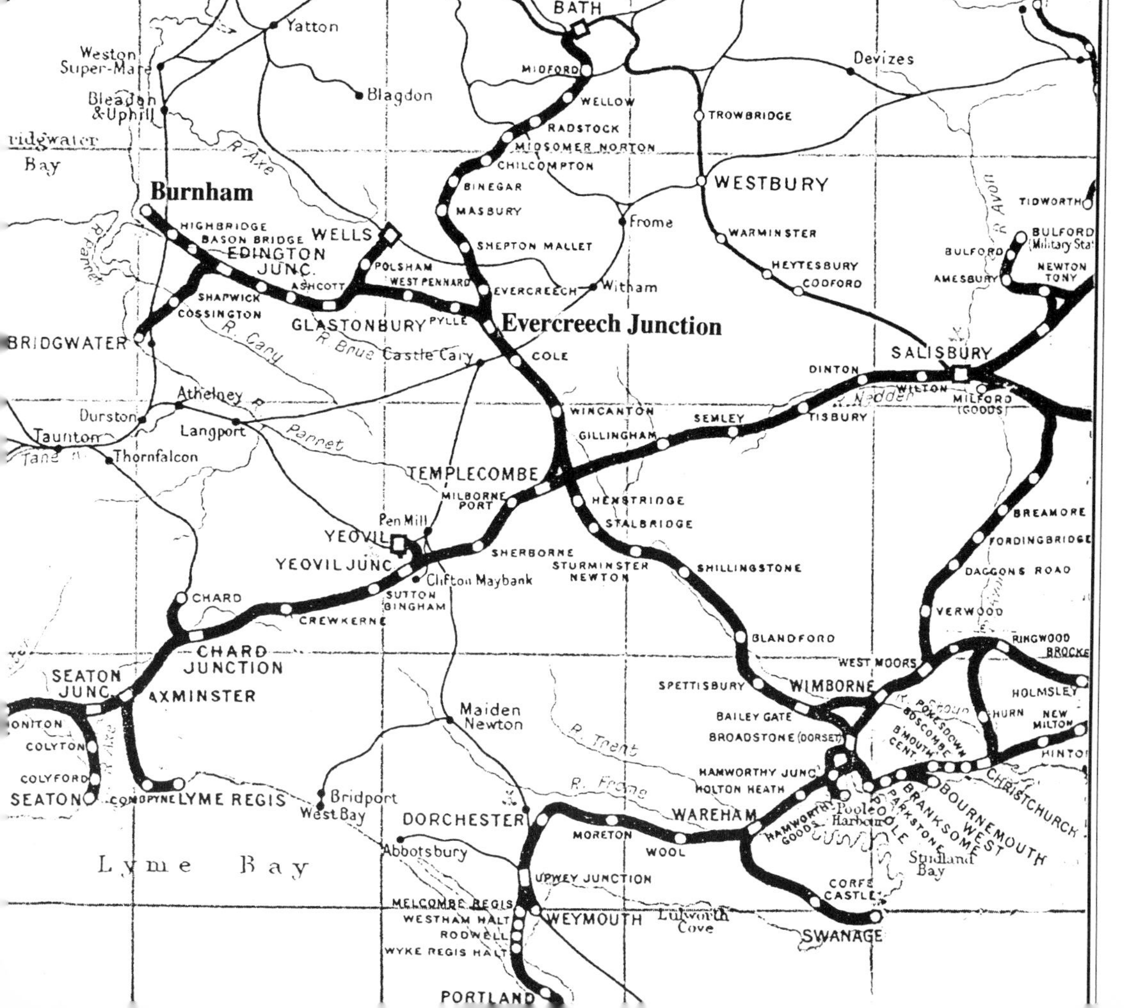

ACKNOWLEDGEMENTS

We are extremely grateful for the assistance received from so many of the photographers mentioned in the captions and also from R. Atthill, W. C. Brown, Dr. P. Cattermole (Museum Curator of the Somerset and Dorset Railway Trust), R. Dagger, S. Ehrlicher, D. Faulkner, The Rev D. Grimwood, C. Handley, W. S. Sampson, N. Stanyon, J. Wilkerson, E. Staff and our ever supportive wives. Tickets have been kindly supplied by G. Croughton, N. Langridge and the SDRT.

The authors and publishers regret that they are not able to supply copies of pictures contained in their publications, but requests for prints of photographs from the Mowat Collection can be made to W. R. Burton, 3 Fairway, Clifton, York and those marked Lens of Sutton can be obtained from 4 Westmead Road, Sutton, Surrey.

GEOGRAPHICAL SETTING

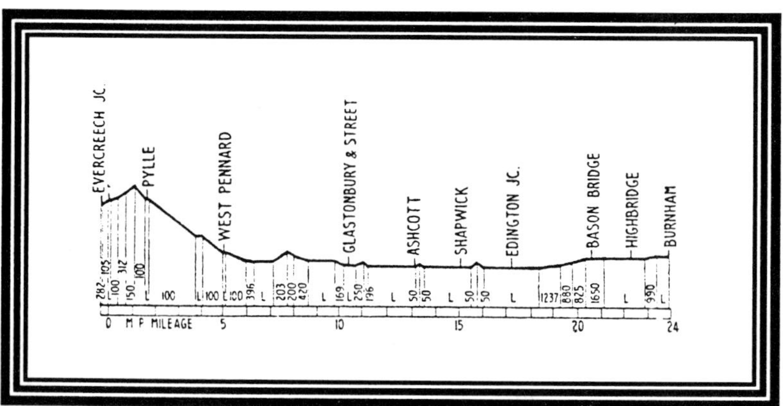

The level area of Somerset is bisected by the Polden Hills which run from Street in the east to Puriton (three miles north of Bridgwater) in the west and rise to about 250 ft above sea level. The railway route ran parallel to, and north of, this ridge which made a scenic feature on the journey. The Bridgwater branch crossed the ridge, west of Cossington.

At Glastonbury, the route skirted the limestone outlier which forms the well known Tor. On Crannel Moor, the branch to Wells diverged. This small ancient city is situated on the southern slope of the Mendip Hills, at about 100 ft above sea level.

The remainder of the route was to the north of Pennard Hill and climbed steadily for three miles before descending into Evercreech Junction.

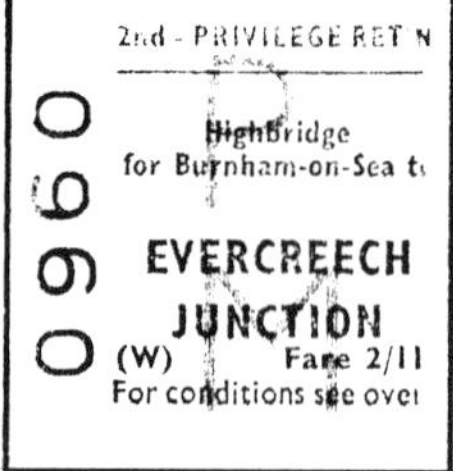

HISTORICAL BACKGROUND

The level area of Somerset has been prone to flooding in winter, its name probably arising from the early **Summer Settlers**. It was across this area of moor that the broad gauge Bristol & Exeter Railway was built, passengers being able to travel between Paddington and Bridgwater from 1841.

Freight transport between Glastonbury and Highbridge by canal commenced on 15th August 1833. This 14 mile waterway, with only one lock, was purchased by the B&ER in 1848 and was closed on 1st July 1854.

The Somerset Central Railway was incorporated in 1852 and was backed by the B&ER who sold the canal to its protege to facilitate the construction of the line between Glastonbury and Highbridge. This broad gauge route was opened to regular traffic on 28th August 1854 and was worked by the B&ER. Extensive wharfage was provided at Highbridge, mainly for use by ships to and from South Wales.

Extension west to Burnham took place on 3rd May 1858 and east to Wells on 15th March 1859.

Further expansion plans involved extension to a south coast harbour so that a South Wales to France service could be offered. This was achieved by the construction of a link from Glastonbury to join the Dorset Central Railway at Bruton. It was opened to Templecombe on 3rd February 1862 as dual gauge, but the broad gauge was little used - probably by only one daily goods train as far south as Evercreech.

The DCR and the SCR were amalgamated to form the Somerset and Dorset Railway on 1st September 1862 and in the following year a Channel to Channel train service commenced.

Over optimism and economic difficulties forced the company into receivership from 1866 until 1870.

In desperation to seek improved revenue, a line across the Mendips to connect with the Midland Railway at Bath was proposed. This was opened from Evercreech Junction on 20th July 1874 and thereafter the Burnham line was regarded as the branch.

The company was soon bankrupt again and was rescued by the joint action of the Midland and London & South Western Railways. Thus the Somerset & Dorset Joint Railway came into being on 13th July 1876. Broad gauge traffic had ceased some years earlier.

The independent Bridgwater Railway was opened from Edington Junction on 21st July 1890 and, although leased by the LSWR, was operated by the SDJR.

In 1923, the SDJR became vested jointly in the SR and LMS. Major changes took place in 1930 when the LMS took over locomotive, commercial and operating matters, while the SR became responsible for civil and signal engineering, together with building maintenance. Coaching stock was provided jointly.

Nationalisation in 1948 brought the route into the Southern Region of British Railways but it was transferred to the Western Region in 1950.

On 29th October 1951 services were withdrawn from the Wells branch and from the Burnham-Highbridge section, although the latter continued to carry a few excursions until 8th September 1962 and freight until 20th May 1963.

The Bridgwater branch was closed to passengers on 1st December 1952 but freight continued to be carried until 4th October 1954. Goods traffic at Bridgwater North continued until 7th July 1962, via a connection with the ex-GWR lines.

The last scheduled trains ran between Highbridge and Evercreech Junction on 5th March 1966, after several previous attempts at closure and amid much opposition. Only the short section of track between Highbridge and Bason Bridge remained in use for milk traffic until 2nd October 1972.

PASSENGER SERVICES

Initially the Bristol & Exeter Railway provided one train which made six journeys between Glastonbury and Highbridge on weekdays and two on Sundays. Upon extension to Wells, the frequency was seven and two respectively. The Burnham section was operated in connection with main line trains and not as an extension of the Wells service, the service being about double that provided on the rest of the route.

The SCR's own service commenced with five trains to Templecombe (with two on Sundays) and five to Wells. The B & E continued to run two broad gauge trains daily to Wells, one of which originated in Bristol. This service lasted until 1868, (as did a broad gauge freight working to Evercreech Junction).

The initial timetable to the Dorset coast showed four trains (two on Sundays) to Poole (Hamworthy). In 1864, an extra train was provided between Highbridge and Glastonbury, in addition to the local service between Burnham and Highbridge.

After the completion of the line to Bath in 1874 the Burnham route became known as "the branch" and there were thereafter few trains to the South Coast. The new timetable showed five trains on the branch, some of which ran to and from Templecombe.

There was little change in the operating pattern until the opening of the Bridgwater branch in 1890. The early timetables showed two trains from Wells, two from Evercreech Junction and two from Templecombe, the latter stopping only twice and giving a good connection from Waterloo. A similar service was operated until 1914 and the timetables were laid out to give the impression that Bridgwater-Templecombe was a main line. During this period there were six or seven trains between Glastonbury and Highbridge with 10 or 12 locals to Wells and to Burnham. From 1927, most of these local trips were operated by push-pull units without a guard.

The table below gives the service frequency on weekdays, Sunday trains having largely ceased by 1890.

1. Highbridge - Evercreech Junction
2. Wells branch
3. Burnham - Highbridge
4. Bridgwater branch

	1	2	3	4
1914	7	10	25	7
1924	8	10	20	10
1934	8	8	18	8
1944	3	3	5	3
1949	5	5	8	5
1954	5	-	-	-
1964	5	-	-	-
1966	2	-	-	-

The 1966 service was an emergency one, operated for only nine weeks, following the failure of the replacement buses to materialise for the planned closure at the end of 1965.

1924

EVERCREECH JUNCTION, GLASTONBURY, and BURNHAM-ON-SEA.—Somerset and Dorset—Southern and L. M. & S.

Miles	Down.	Week Days only. mrn	mrn	mrn	non	b	c	aft	aft	aft		aft	aft
	Evercreech Junction† dep.	....	8 15	1015	....	1250	3 37	4 55	6 45	....	...	9 20	10s10
1½	Pylle	....	8 21	1021	....	1256	3 43	5 1	6 51	....	...	9 26	10s16
5	West Pennard	....	8 27	1028	....	1 3	3 49	5 7	6 57	....	...	9 32	10s22
10¼	Glastonbury §§ arr.	....	8 35	1036	....	1 11	3 57	5 15	7 5	....	...	9 40	10s30
—	Mls Wells (Priory Rd.) dep.	6 55	8 15	9 55	1145	1255	3 45	5 0	6 40	8 15	...	9 27	10s15
—	2½ Polsham	7 5	8 20	10 0	1150	1 0	3 50	5 5	6 49	8 20	...	9 32	10s20
—	5½ Glastonbury §§ arr.	7 11	8 26	10 6	1156	1 6	3 56	5 11	6 59	8 26	...	9 38	10s26
	Glastonbury §§ dep.	7 40	8 38	1041	....	1 15	4 0	5 18	7 8	8 35	...	9 44	....
13	Ashcott §	7 46	8 44	1047	....	1 21	4 6	5 24	....	8 41	...	9 50	....
15	Shapwick ‡	7 51	8 49	1051	....	1 26	4 11	5 29	....	8 52	...	9 55	....
17¼	Edington Junction 165 arr.	7 56	8 53	1056	....	1 30	4 15	5 33	7 18	8 56	...	9 59	....
	dep.	8 4	8 55	11 2	....	1 32	4 17	5 34	7 20	8 58	...	10 0	....
20¼	Bason Bridge	8 11	9 2	11 9	....	1 39	4 24	5 41	7 27	9 6	...	10 7	....
22¼	Highbridge * arr.	8 16	9 6	1113	....	1 43	4 28	5 45	7 31	9 10	...	1011	....
	dep.	8 27	9 8	1126	....	1 47	4 31	5 55	7 40	9 15	...	1015	....
24	Burnham-on-Sea arr.	8 32	9 13	1131	....	1 52	4 36	6 0	7 45	9 20	...	1020	....

Miles	Up.	Week Days only. mrn	mrn	mrn	mrn	mrn	aft	aft	aft	aft	aft	aft	aft
	Burnham-on-Sea dep.	....	....	....	9 25	1120	....	3 10	5 5	6 30	8 25	....	Saturdays only.
1¾	Highbridge * arr.	....	....	....	9 30	1125	....	3 15	5 10	6 35	8 30	....	
	dep.	6 45	7 7	....	9 40	1130	....	3 20	5 20	6 45	8 32	....	
3¾	Bason Bridge	n	h	....	9 45	1135	....	3 26	5 25	....	8 37	....	
6¾	Edington Junction 165 arr.	6 53	h	....	9 51	1141	....	3 32	5 31	6 53	8 43	....	
	dep.	6 55	....	....	9 56	1143	....	3 35	5 35	6 55	8 45	....	
9	Shapwick ‡	n	h	....	10 1	1148	....	3 41	5 40	....	8 53	....	
11	Ashcott §	n	h	....	10 6	1153	....	3 46	5 45	....	8 58	....	
13¼	Glastonbury §§ arr.	7 9	7 31	....	1011	1158	....	3 51	5 50	7 6	9 3	....	
—	Glastonbury §§ dep.	....	7 45	8 40	1045	1210	1 20	4 5	5 55	7 15	9 8	9 50	1040
16¾	Polsham	....	....	8 47	1053	1218	1 28	4 13	6 3	7 23	9 16	9 58	1048
19¼	Wells ‖ arr.	....	8 0	8 52	1054	1223	1 33	4 18	6 8	7 28	9 21	10 3	1053
—	Glastonbury §§ dep.	7 14	....	....	1017	12 7	....	3 59	5 54	7 16	....	....	....
19	West Pennard	7 25	....	....	1027	1219	....	4 9	6 3	7 25	....	....	....
22¼	Pylle [305, 306	7 34	....	....	1035	1227	....	4 17	6 11	7 33	....	....	....
24	Evercreech Junc. † arr.	7 39	....	....	1041	1232	....	4 22	6 16	7 38	....	....	....

b Through Train from Bournemouth, see page 306.
c Through Train from Templecombe, see page 306.
h Stops when required.
n Stops to take up for beyond Glastonbury.
s Saturdays only.
* Adjoining G. W. Station.
† Station for Castle Cary (3 miles).
‡ Station for Westhay (1 mile).
§ Station for Meare (1¼ mile).
§§ Glastonbury and Street.
‖ Priory Road; about ¼ mile to Tucker Street Station.

Sec. and Gen. Man., Robert A. Read.]

SOMERSET and DORSET.

ne classes refer to the merset & Dorset Line only.	1&2	1,2,3	1&2	1&2	1&2	1&2	1&2	1&2	1&2	1&2
	mrn	a	mrn	mrn	mrn	aft	aft	aft	aft	aft
urnham ... dep		8 10	9 0	....	1135	1 15	2 10	4 0	7 50	8 40
ighbridge 9, 10 ... arr		8 16	9 6	....	1140	1 20	2 16	4 6	7 56	8 47
8 Birmnghm (New St.) dep		2 45	....	....	....	9 5	Stop	9 55		4 50
9 Bristol ... ,,		6 30	....	....	1030	1235		3 15		8 10
0 Exeter (St. David's) ,,		....	6 0	....	10 0	1225		....		5 30
ighbridge ... dep		8 24	9 10	....	1155	1 55		4 30		9 0
ason Brdg. (fr Woolavington & Cossington		8 29	....	....	....	....		....		9 5
dington		8 38	9 24	....	1215	....		4 45		9 14
hapwck (fr Wsthay & Meare		8 44	9 30	....	1222	b		4 53		9 20
shcot and Meare ...		8 49	h	....	....	....		....		9 25
lastonbury ... arr		8 57	9 42	....	1236	2 15		5 5		9 32
Brnch Glastonbury ... dep		....	9 45	11 0	1240	2 20		5 8		9 35
Brnch Polsham ...		....	9 54	11 9	b	....		h		9 44
Brnch Wells 7 ... arr		....	10 0	1115	1252	2 35		5 20		9 50
lastonbury ... dep		9 0			Stop	2 17		5 29		....
est Pennard ...		9 12			....	....		5 40		....
ylle (for Shepton Mallet)		9 23			....	b		5 55		....
vercreech (for Ditcheat) ..		9 30			....	....		6 5		....
ole (for Bruton & Castle C.)		9 38			....	2 49		6 20		....
incanton ...		9 50			....	2 59		6 45		....
emple Combe J. 38, 35 arr		10 0			....	3 5		7 0		....
8 Exeter (Queen St.) arr		1 20			....	5 50		9 45		....
8 Southampton ... ,,		1256			....	5 41	1&2	9 32		....
5 London (Waterloo). ,,		2 13			....	6 53	aft	1113		....
emple Combe (S.W. Sta.) d	8s10	1012			....	3s8	3 40	7 40		....
enstridge ...	8 17	1022			....	....	4 5	h		....
albridge ...	8 22	1027			....	....	4 15	7 57		....
urminster Newton ...	8 3	1039			1&2	b	4 35	8 8		....
hillingstone 1 ...	8 43	1047			aft	h	4 50	8 16		....
landford ...	9 0	11 5			1 0	3 38	5 15	8 28		....
etisbury ... (Marshall)	9 9	1114			1 9	....	5 25	8 36		....
ailey Gate (for Sturminster	9 20	1122			1 17	....	5 34	8 42		....
imborne Junc. 34 ... arr	9 32	1137			1 30	4 0	5 50	8 54		....
Southampton 34 ... arr	1124	2 53			2 53	....	7 9	1257		....
London (Waterloo) 35 ,,	2 35	5 42			5 42	....	1010	4 7		....
imborne ... dep	9 36	1140			1 45	4 2	6 10	9 5		....
oole Junction 33 ...	9 50	1155			2 0	4 15	6 25	9 20		....
oole (for Bournemouth) ar	9 55	12 0			2 5	4 20	6 30	9 25		....

a 3rd class to Stations between Wimborne and London, via Wimborne.

d 3rd class to Bristol and Exeter down Stations, leaving Highbridge at 9 52 mrn.

j Sets down from South Western Stations, or take up for Bristol and Exeter or Midland Stations.

1, Station for Child Okeford and Okeford Fitzpain.

f 3rd class from Weymouth & intermediate Stations, via Wimborne, & from Exeter & intermediate Stations, via Temple Combe, to Stations on this Line.

Frm Weymouth, Dorchester, &c., see p. 7.	1&2	1,2,3	1&2	1,2,3	1&2	1&2	1&2	1&2	1&2	1,2,3	1&2	1&2	1&2
	mrn	mrn	mrn	c	mrn	f	mrn	e	aft	aft	aft	aft	aft
Poole ... dep	e	d	d	8 5		1045	....	1 20	....	....	5 25	7 0	8 40
Poole Junction ...			....	8 10		1050	....	1 25	....	....	5 30	7 5	8 45
Wimborne ... arr			....	8 25		11 5	....	1 40	....	....	5 45	7 20	9 0
32 London (Watrloo) d			....	....		....	8 15	8 15	....	....	....	3 10	....
33 Southampton ,,			....	6 8		....	1056	1056	....	....	....	5 34	....
Wimborne ... dep			....	8 30		1110	1220	1 50	....	....	6 5	7 25	9 5
Bailey Gate ...			....	8 42		1122	1235	2 2	....	....	....	7 40	9 17
Spetisbury ...			....	8 50		....	1242	2 10	....	....	....	7 50	9 25
Blandford ...			....	9 5		1135	1250	2 23	....	....	6 32	8 0	9 36
Shillingstone 1 ...			....	9 20		1147	Stop	2 37	....	....	6 45	8 20	9 50
Sturminster Newton .			....	9 29		1154		2 45	....	....	6 54	8 33	9 58
Stalbridge ...			....	9 41		12 4		2 57	....	....	7 5	8 45	1010
Henstridge ... [38			....	9 46		....		3 2	....	....	7 10	8 50	1015
Temple Combe J. 35, a			....	9 55		1218		3 20	....	....	7 25	8 55	1020
32 London (Watrloo) d			....	....	6 45	....		1140	....	....	3 50	Except Mondays.	Mondays only.
38 Southampton ,,			....	....	8 30	....		1250	....	....	4 50		
38 Exeter (Queen St) ,,			....	....	7 45	10 5		1 30	....	....	5 0		
Temple Cmb (S.W. Sta			7s10	9s55	1110	1226		3 40	....	....	7 45		
Wincanton ...			7 22	10 2	1125	1238		3 51	....	....	8 0		
Cole ...			7 35	1014	1140	1248		4 3	....	....	8 15		
Evercreech ...			7 45	1022	j	....		4 11	....	....	8 25		
Pylle ...			7 53	1028	j	i		4 17	....	....	8 31		
West Pennard ...			8 5	1035	j	....		4 25	....	....	8 44		
Glastonbury ... arr			8 20	1048	1230	1 16		4 36	....	....	9 0		
Wells Brnch Wells ... dep		7 35	....	1035	1215	1 0		4 20	....	7 10	....		
Wells Brnch Polsham ...		7 40	....	1040	....	....		h	....	7 15	. .		
Wells Brnch Glastonbury arr		7 47	....	1046	1227	1 14		4 34	....	7 22	....		
Glastonbury ... dep		7 50	8 30	1052	1230	1 20		4 40	....	7 25	9 5		
Ashcot and Meare ...		7 58	....	....	....	....		. .	....	7 32	....		
Shapwick ...		8 3	....	11 4	1250	....		4 53	....	7 37	9 20		
Edington ...		8 9	....	....	j	....		4 58	....	7 42	....		
Bason Bridge ...		8 19	....	....	....	. .		....	....	7 52	....		
Highbridge 9, 10 arr		8 24	9 5	1120	1 15	1 45		5 10	....	7 57	9 36		
9 Exetr (St. Dvids) a		1230	1230	1 25	3 10	6 35		9 15	....	1020	....	....	....
Bristol 10 ... ,,		9 50	....	1240	2 35	2 35	1&2	6 29	....	9 30	....	....	....
171 Brmnghm Nw. St. ,,		3 20	....	6 10	6 35	6 49	aft	1018	....	....	....	....	....
Highbridge ... dep	7 52	8 40	....	1155	1 54	1 54	3 25	5 20	7 6	8 10	....	....	....
Burnham ... arr	8 0	8 46	....	12 0	2 0	2 0	3 30	5 25	7 12	8 15	....	....	....

e 3rd class from London only to Stations on this Line, via Temple Combe.

b Stops to set down from, or take up for, foreign Stations only.

s Depart from the Lower Station at Temple Combe.

f 3rd class from South Western Stations.

i Stops to set down on informing the Guard.

h Stops by signal when required.

a 3rd class from all Somerset and Dorset Stations to all Stations on the London and South Western Line, via Temple Combe; and, via Wimborne, to all Stations between Wimborne & Weymouth. c 3rd class from Southampton & intermediate Stations, via Wimborne, & from Salisbury and intermediate Stations via Temple Combe, to Stations on this Line; also from all Somerset & Dorset Stations to Stas. on the Bristol & Exeter & Midland Lines, leaving Highbridge at 11 48 mrn.

BURNHAM-ON-SEA and EVERCREECH JUNC.—Somerset & Dorset—Southern and L. M. & S.

Miles	Down.	Week Days only.																				
		mrn		a	c		c		aft		aft	aft		aft		aft		aft		aft	aft	
	Burnham-on-Sea ... dep.	..	..	8 8	9 55	..	1120	..	..	..	1 50	3 0	..	..	..	5 20	..	6 30	..	8 35	9 50	..
	Highbridge A 14, 20 arr	..	..	8 13	10 0	..	1127	..	..	..	1 58	3 5	..	..	..	5 25	..	6 35	..	8 40	9 55	..
1¼	Highbridge A 14, 20 dep	6 40	..	8 15	10 3	..	1135	..	..	..	..	3 15	..	..	..	..	..	6 45	..	8 41	..	..
3½	Bason Bridge ...	6 44	..	8 19	10 7	..	1142	..	..	..	..	3 19	..	..	..	..	..	6 49	..	8 46	..	..
6¼	Edington Junction (below) arr.	6 51	..	8 26	1014	..	1149	..	..	..	..	3 26	..	..	..	..	..	6 56	..	8 53	..	..
	Edington Junction (below) dep.	6 52	..	8 27	1015	..	1150	..	..	..	..	3 27	..	..	..	..	..	6 57	..	8 54	..	..
9	Shapwick B ...	6 57	..	8 33	1021	..	1156	..	..	..	..	3 33	..	..	..	..	..	7 3	..	9 0	..	..
11	Ashcott C ...	7 2	..	8 38	1026	..	12 1	..	..	..	..	3 38	..	..	..	..	..	7 8	..	9 5	..	..
13¼	Glastonbury D ... arr	7 9	..	8 45	1033	..	12 8	..	..	..	..	3 45	..	..	..	..	..	7 15	..	9 13	..	..
—	Glastonbury D ... dep.	..	..	9 5	1040	..	..	..	1 10	..	..	4 20	..	5 20	..	..	..	..	..	9 15	..	..
16¾	Polsham Halt ...	..	..	9 13	1046	..	..	..	1 16	..	..	4 26	..	5 26	..	..	..	..	..	9 22	..	..
19½	Wells F 51 ... arr.	..	..	9 23	1052	..	..	..	1 22	..	..	4 32	..	5 32	..	..	..	..	..	9 28	..	..
—	Glastonbury D ... dep.	7 10	..	..	1037	..	1210	..	..	..	..	3 50	..	..	..	..	..	7 20	..	..	..	..
19	West Pennard ...	7 21	..	..	1047	..	1220	..	..	..	..	4 0	..	..	..	..	..	7 29	..	..	..	..
22¼	Pylle ... [1076, 1077	7 29	..	..	1055	..	1228	..	..	..	..	4 8	..	..	..	..	..	7 37	..	..	..	..
24	Evercreech Junc. G arr.	7 35	..	..	11 1	..	1234	..	..	..	..	4 15	..	..	..	..	..	7 44	..	..	..	..

Miles	Up.	Week Days only.																					
		mrn		mrn		mrn		c		aft		c		aft		aft		aft		aft		aft	
	Evercreech Junction . dep.	a	..	8 15	..	10 5	..	1238	..	..	..	3 48	..	4 50	..	..	..	..	..	8 10	..	9 20	..
1¾	Pylle ...	..	..	8 20	..	1010	..	1244	..	..	..	3 54	..	4 55	..	..	..	..	..	8 15	..	..	..
5	West Pennard ...	..	..	8 28	..	1017	..	1252	..	..	..	4 1	..	5 2	..	..	..	..	..	8 22	..	9 30	..
10¾	Glastonbury D ... arr.	..	..	8 39	..	1027	..	1 2	..	..	..	4 12	..	5 12	..	..	..	..	..	8 32	..	9 42	..
—	Mls Wells F ... dep.	6 55	..	..	..	1015	..	1250	..	..	..	3 35	..	5 0	..	6 45	..	..	..	..	..	..	..
—	2¾ Polsham Halt ...	7 0	..	..	..	1020	..	..	..	..	..	3 40	..	5 5	..	6 52	..	..	..	..	..	..	..
—	5¾ Glastonbury D arr.	7 7	..	..	..	1027	..	1 2	..	..	..	3 47	..	5 12	..	7 3	..	..	..	..	..	..	..
—	Glastonbury D ... dep.	7 20	..	8 45	..	1033	..	1 8	..	..	..	4 14	..	5 15	..	..	..	..	..	8 35	..	9 46	..
13	Ashcott C ...	7 26	..	8 52	..	1040	..	1 15	..	..	..	4 21	..	5 22	..	..	..	..	..	8 42	..	Xx	..
15	Shapwick B ...	7 31	..	8 57	..	1046	..	1 21	..	..	..	4 26	..	5 27	..	..	..	..	..	8 47	..	Xx	..
17¾	Edington Junction (below) arr.	7 37	..	9 4	..	1052	..	1 27	..	..	..	4 32	..	5 33	..	..	..	..	..	8 54	..	Xx	..
	Edington Junction (below) dep.	7 38	..	9 5	..	1053	..	1 28	..	..	..	4 33	..	5 34	..	..	..	..	..	8 55	..	..	..
20¼	Bason Bridge ...	7 45	..	9 12	..	11 0	..	1 35	..	..	..	4 42	..	5 41	..	..	..	..	..	9 2	..	..	..
22¾	Highbridge A 14, 20 arr.	7 50	..	9 17	..	11 5	..	1 40	..	..	..	4 47	..	5 46	..	..	..	..	..	9 10	..	1015	..
	Highbridge A 14, 20 dep.	7 55	..	9 20	..	1110	..	1 43	..	245	..	5 5	..	5 55	..	..	..	8 25	..	9 30	..	1020	..
24	Burnham-on-Sea ... arr.	8 0	..	9 25	..	1115	..	1 48	..	250	..	5 10	..	6 0	..	.	..	8 30	..	9 35	..	1025	..

A Adjoining G. W. Sta. a Third cl. only. B Sta. for Westhay (1 ml.) C Sta. for Meare (1¼ mile). c Thro Trains to and from Templecombe, pages 1076 and 1077. D Glastonbury and Street. F Priory Road. G Sta. for Castle Cary (3 mls.) Xx Sets down on informing Guard.

BRIDGWATER and EDINGTON (3rd class only).—Somerset & Dorset—Southern and L. M. & S.

Miles	Down.	mrn	mrn	mrn	aft	aft	aft	aft	aft
	Bridgwater ... dep.	8 5	9 50	1130	1 5	2 55	5 10	6 30	8 30
3	Bawdrip Halt ...	8 10	9 55	1135	1 10	3 0	5 15	6 35	8 35
4½	Cossington ... [above	8 14	9 59	1139	1 14	3 4	5 19	6 39	8 39
7¼	Edington Junction arr.	8 21	10 6	1146	1 21	3 11	5 26	6 46	8 46

Miles	Up.	mrn	mrn	W	mrn	aft	aft	aft	aft	aft
	Edington Junc. ... dep.	7 38	8 30	9 10	1055	1 30	4 35	5 35	7 0	9 0
3	Cossington ...	Xx	8 36	..	11 1	1 36	4 41	5 41	7 6	9 6
4½	Bawdrip Halt ... [20	..	8 40	..	11 5	1 41	4 45	5 45	7 10	9 10
7¼	Bridgwater K 14, arr.	7 53	8 46	9 30	1111	1 46	4 51	5 51	7 16	9 16

K Sta. for Spaxton. W Weds. only. Xx Sets down on informing Guard.

BURNHAM-ON-SEA

1. The terminus at the select Georgian resort of about 2000 residents was graced with an overall roof, a type employed at important locations by the early railway builders and rare over S&DR metals. By the turn of the century there were over 5000 inhabitants. (D. Cullum coll.)

3. Prior to the bus era, a frequent service was operated to Highbridge to give connection with GWR services and to convey employees to the SDJR's works. A crooked snap is worth including to show the Sentinel steam railcar used for a short while. This was one of 13 purchased by the LMS between 1925 and 1927. LSWR railmotor no. 1 was also used unsuccessfully in 1906. (A. Vaughan coll.)

This plan was included with the documents deposited before Parliament in 1855 and shows the proposed pier. (SDRT)

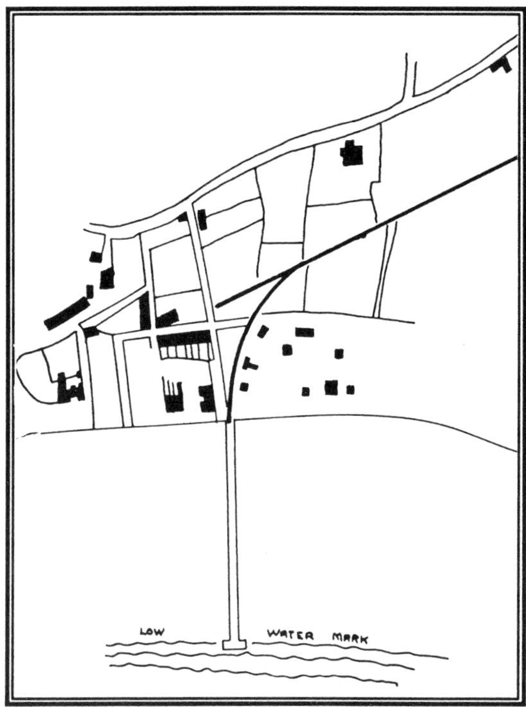

←

2. The cleanliness of 0-6-0 no. 28 and its coaches is evident in this 1895 view, which includes the 30 cwt goods crane and the elevated locomotive water tank. Beneath this, four men worked repairing the sails of the company's ships and producing wagon sheets. Driver Hill and Fireman Braund were based at Highbridge. A weekly season ticket between the two towns was available at a cost of 6d. (SDRT / R. Atthill coll.)

1924

HIGHBRIDGE and BURNHAM-ON-SEA.—Somerset and Dorset—Southern and L. M. & S.

Miles	Down.	Week Days only.																													
		mrn	mrn	mrn	mrn	mrn		mrn	mrn		aft	aft	aft		aft	aft	aft		aft	aft	aft		aft	aft	aft	aft					
	Highbridge ....dep.	7 25	8 0	8 27	9 8	10 5	....	1050	1126	....	1230	1 47	2 45	....	4 15	4 31	5 25	....	5 55	6 50	7 40	....	8 15	9 15	9 40	1015	....	....	....	....	....
1¼	Burnham-on-Sea ....arr.	7 30	8 5	8 32	9 13	1010	....	1055	1131	....	1235	1 52	2 50	....	4 20	4 36	5 30	....	6 0	6 55	7 45	....	8 20	9 20	9 45	1020	....	....	....	....	....

Miles	Up.	Week Days only.																													
		mrn	mrn	mrn	mrn	mrn		mrn	aft	aft		aft	aft		aft	aft	aft	aft	aft		aft	aft	aft	aft	aft						
	Burnham-on-Sea ....dep.	7 45	8 10	8 40	9 25	1015	....	1120	1215	1 25	....	2 20	3 10	....	4 45	5 5	5 40	6 30	7 20	....	7 55	8 25	9 25	9 50	1025	....	....	....	....	....	....
1¼	Highbridge * ....arr.	7 50	8 15	8 45	9 30	1020	....	1125	1220	1 30	....	2 25	3 15	....	4 50	5 10	5 45	6 35	7 25	....	8 0	8 30	9 30	9 55	1030	....	....	....	....	....	....

* Adjoining G. W. Station.

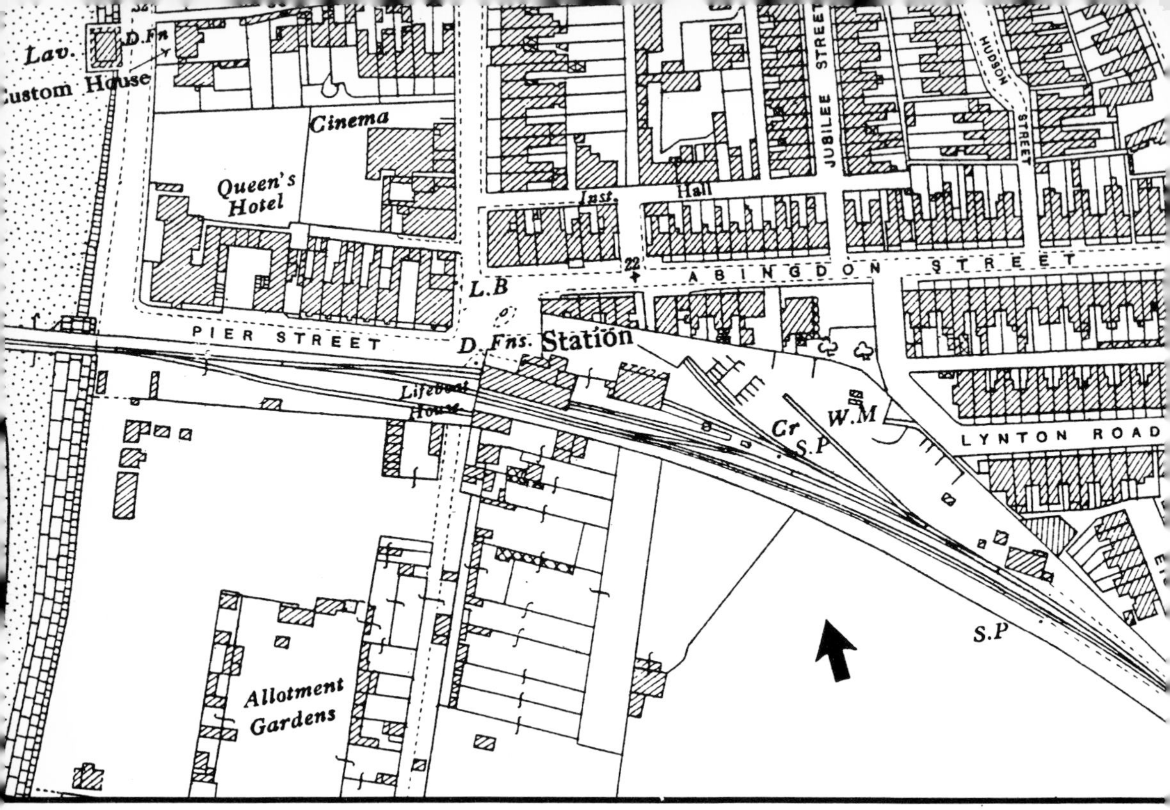

The 1930 survey shows the layout which had probably remained unchanged for at least 60 years. The pier on the left had been used by the SDJR's own passenger steamers but it was sold in 1905.

4. On the right is the lifeboat station which was once rail connected (see map). The boat was kept on a rail vehicle and launched down the 1 in 23 gradient of the stone pier. The building became a scout hut in 1937 and was still in use as such in 1989. (Lens of Sutton)

5. The excursion platform was 225 yds long while the covered down platform was only 88 yds. The suffix "on-sea" was added by the SR in June 1923 to attract passengers. The water tank had been removed by the time this photograph was taken in October 1950. (D. Clayton)

6. To mark the centenary of the SCR, a special train of 12 coaches was hauled by 0-6-0 no. 43201 (formerly SDJR no. 64) on 28th August 1954. It carried over 600 passengers, about 100 of whom were descendents of James Clark, one of the founders of the SCR and of the famous Glastonbury shoe making firm. (C. L. Caddy coll.)

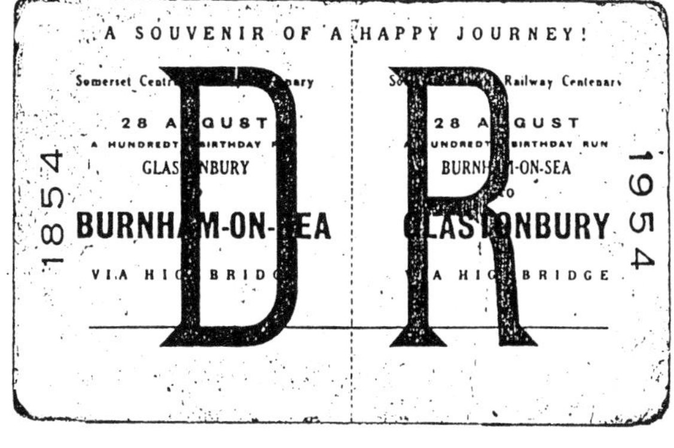

7. The crossover points were worked by the lever between the tracks but release was controlled from the signal box. Road improvements have obliterated the station site and much of the trackbed, while a Gateway supermarket occupies the area on the left. (SDRT)

8. On 22nd August 1959, class 3F no. 43427 was to be found with empty stock. Summer excursion trains visited Burnham-on-Sea from the end of regular services on 29th October 1951 until 8th September 1962. The signal box contained four levers and has been relocated at the Somerset & Dorset Railway Trust's Museum at Washford. (R. E. Toop)

9. Ex-GWR 0-6-0 no. 2204 stands on the foot crossing to the excursion platform, having arrived with the 1.15pm special from Evercreech Junction on 21st July 1962. Traffic ceased totally when freight facilities were withdrawn on 20th May 1963. (E. Wilmshurst)

RAILWAY SHIPPING FLEET

Name	Type	Tonnage Gross/Net	Registered Owner	Pass. / Cargo
RUBY	Iron Paddler	155/98	Burnham Tidal Harbour Co.	P
DEFIANCE	Iron Paddler	150/96	Burnham Tidal Harbour Co.	P
HEATHER BELL	Iron Paddler	152/95	Burnham Tidal Harbour Co.	P
GEORGE REED	Iron Screw	170/115	George Reed (for BTH Co.)	P
RAILWAY	Wood Ketch	59	Somerset & Dorset	C
JULIA	Wood Ketch	69	Somerset & Dorset	C
RICHARD & EMILY	Wood Ketch	82	Somerset & Dorset	C
LEOPARD	Iron Screw	67/42	Somerset & Dorset	C
ALPHA	Iron Screw	82/48*	Somerset & Dorset Joint	C
SHERBRO	Wood Paddler	239/119	Somerset & Dorset Joint	P
JULIA (2)	Steel Screw	197/78	Somerset & Dorset Joint	C
RADSTOCK	Steel Screw	195/78	Somerset & Dorset Joint	C

* ALPHA was twice lengthened making her tonnage 94/55 and 111/76.

HIGHBRIDGE WHARF

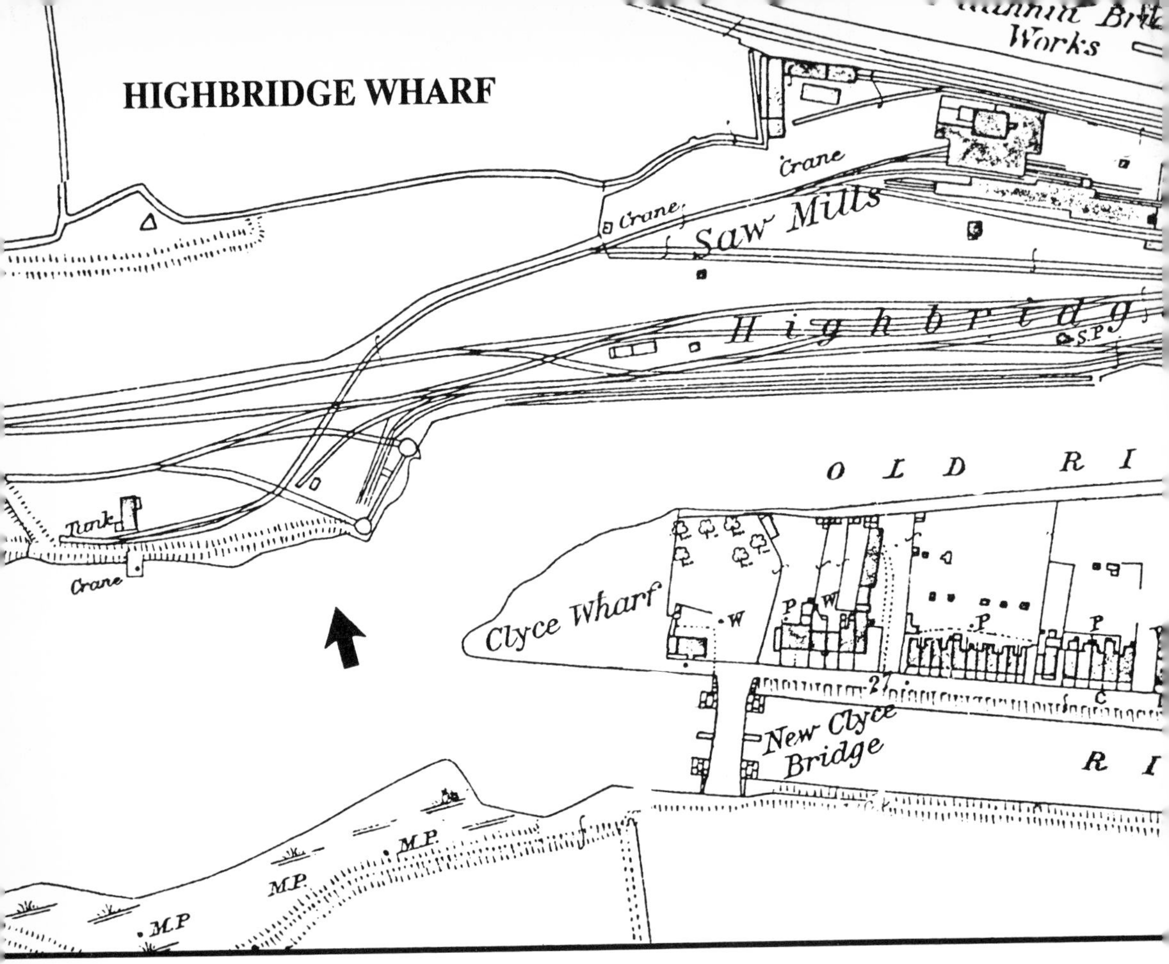

Top left on this 1888 map is the line from Burnham, from which sidings on the south side served Apex Brickworks and Colthurst, Symons Brickworks. Church Street level crossing is on the extreme right.

10. The wharf was at the western end of the Glastonbury Canal and came under railway control when it ws purchased by the B&ER. The SDJR's ships operated from here until the last was sold in 1933. (A. Vaughan coll.)

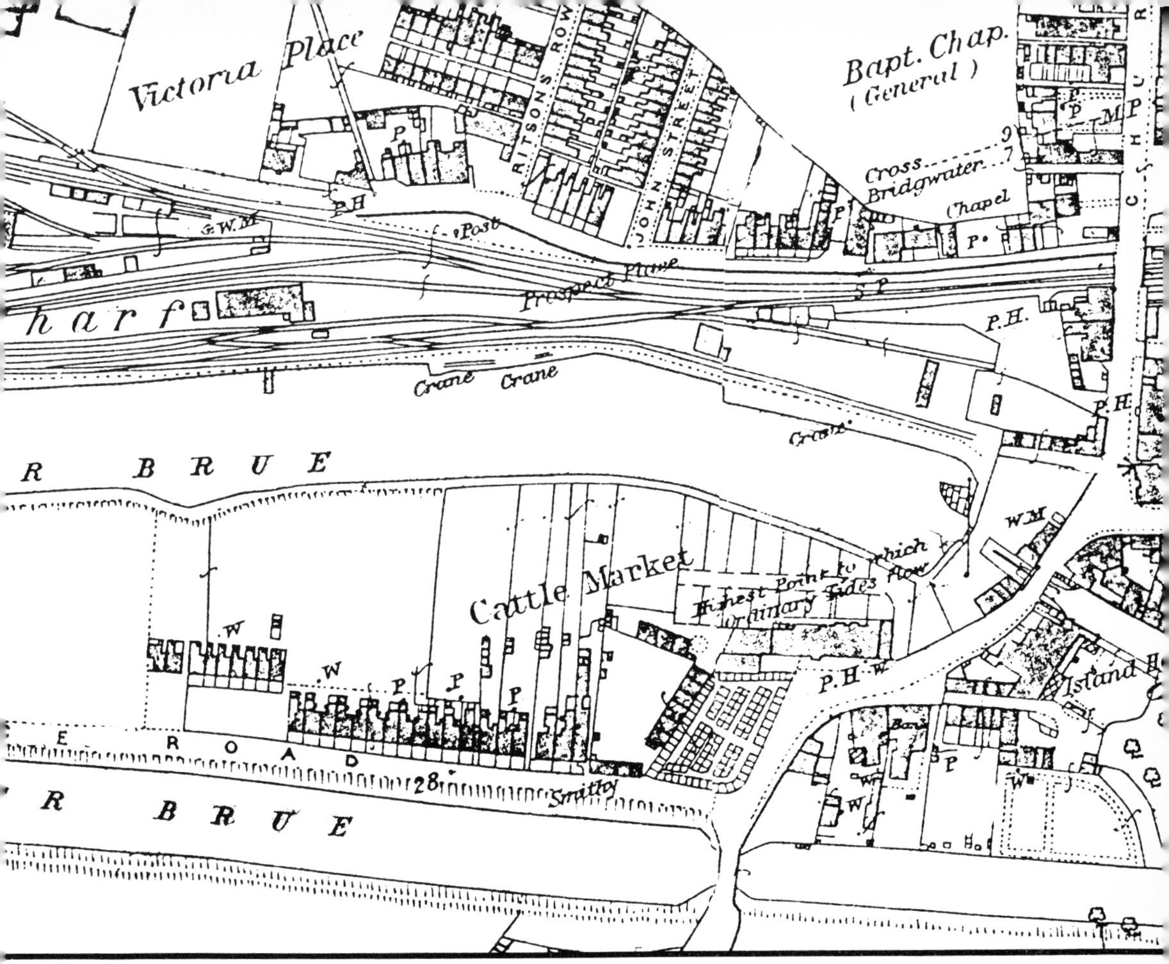

11. Vast tonnages of rail were shipped from South Wales for use on the SDJR and the LSWR. Goods in the return direction included much Somerset dairy and agricultural produce. (A. Vaughan coll.)

12. Timber was landed in large quantities for well over a century, non-railway owned ships continuing to use the wharf until its closure on 2nd November 1964. The entire basin has now been infilled. (A. Vaughan coll.)

13. A westward view from the footbridge adjacent to the Church Street level crossing includes the extensive cattle pens. For some years a siding curved sharply, across the canal lock, to reach the cattle market. Seen when described as Highbridge "C" Box, the structure was redesignated "East A" by BR and closed on 16th May 1965, when the wharf sidings closed. (Mowat coll.)

HIGHBRIDGE (GWR)

14. The line from Burnham and Highbridge "B" Box is on the left, the GWR goods yard and line to Bristol being the main features. A siding to a brickworks diverged from the loop on the right. The wooden post on the left carries a GWR backing arm, with two holes in it. (Mowat coll.)

15. The designation of the 12-lever "B" Box was changed to "East B", its main functions being the control of the access to the S & D goods yard and the level crossing gates over the road to the GWR goods yard. The signals shown were selected by West Box (ex GWR), seen in the background of this July 1964 photograph. East B box closed on 16th May 1965. (J. J. Smith)

The Grange
S.P.
S.P.
S.P.
S.P.
S.P.
Crane
S.B.
S.P.
Railway Hotel
S.B.
W
S.B.
S.B.
F.B.
MARKET STREET
Station
Huish Rhyne
Huish Rhyne
Island House
Old River Brue
S.P.

top left

16. West Box controlled the passage of S&D line trains over the Bristol main line and was closed on 20th March 1972. The connection between the two routes is on the right of this 1962 picture, the line to the former GWR goods yard being on the lower left. (E. Wilmshurst)

17. LMS no. 1370 rattles over the crossing on 13th July 1935 as it approaches the S&D platforms on its way from Burnham-on-Sea. Occasional excursions from Weston-super-Mare were obliged to reverse round the curve on the left and then pass over the crossing. In 1965, the disused Burnham line was slewed into the goods yard. (S. W. Baker)

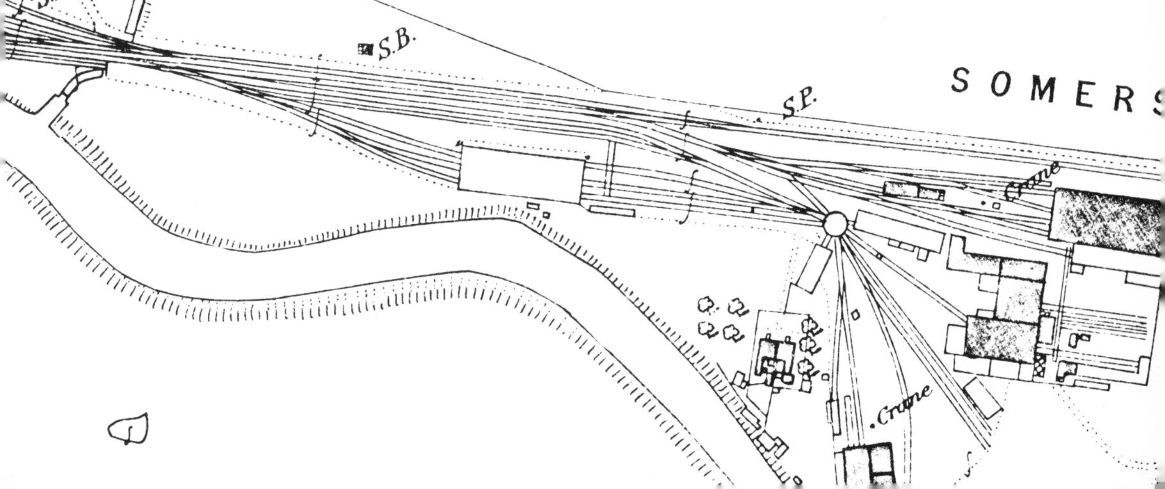

On the left page of this 1888 map are the goods sheds of the GWR (top) and the SDJR (left), the separate roadways to their passenger stations also being marked. On the right is the SDJR Locomotive and Carriage Works.

HIGHBRIDGE (S&D)

18. The former SCR station and terminal platforms are on the right and a flight of steps to the road bridge is near the centre. This is shown on the 1888 map together with a similar flight on the other side of the bridge. No footbridge over the SDJR was shown then, an iron one being erected in 1896. (Lens of Sutton)

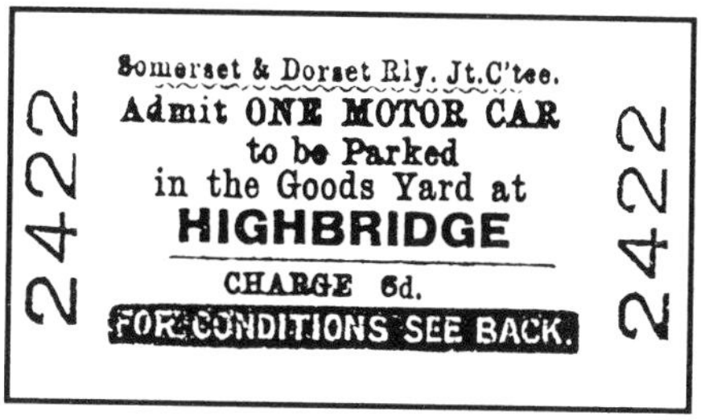

2422

Somerset & Dorset Rly. Jt.C'tee.
Admit ONE MOTOR CAR
to be Parked
in the Goods Yard at
HIGHBRIDGE

CHARGE 6d.
FOR CONDITIONS SEE BACK.

2422

19. "A" Box ceased to be used in 1914 when control of the crossing was transferred to the GWR West Box, which was then extended and its roofline altered. The footbridge of iron, with wooden panels on the approaches, was replaced by a reinforced concrete structure, in about 1933. (Lens of Sutton)

20. The 6.45pm to Evercreech Junction on 22nd September 1928 was hauled by no. 55, built by Vulcan Foundry in 1884. It was amongst the first SDJR locomotives to be built with a complete cab. (K. Nunn / LCGB)

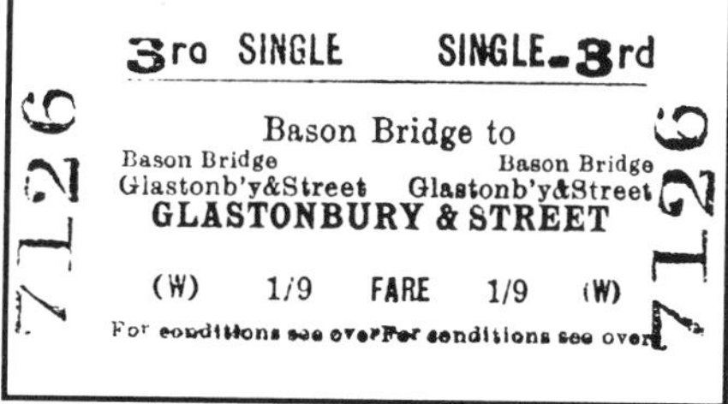

7126

3rd SINGLE SINGLE-3rd

Bason Bridge to
Bason Bridge Bason Bridge
Glastonb'y&Street Glastonb'y&Street
GLASTONBURY & STREET

(W) 1/9 FARE 1/9 (W)
For conditions see over For conditions see over

7126

21. The 8.20am Evercreech Junction to Highbridge has just arrived at platform 5 on 4th August 1952. Behind it is the former carriage and wagon erecting shop and beyond that is the

SDJR locomotive works. A 3-road carriage shed once stood behind the signal box. (J. J. Smith)

22. Platform 1 is on the right and 0-6-0 no. 43248 is standing at platforms 2 and 3 with the 2.20pm to Templecombe on 7th July 1959. Platform 4 is on the down through line and was linked to 5, 6 and 7 by the SR footbridge in the background. The former "A" Box had been retained as a staff room. "For Burnham-on-Sea" was added in 1951. (R. C. Riley)

HIGHBRIDGE

23. After the withdrawal of passenger services to Burnham, the terminal platforms saw more traffic than previously. This view from the steps to the road includes the bronze war memorial panel, formerly situated in the locomotive works. "East C" Box is in the distance. (Lens of Sutton)

24. "East C" Box was "Loco Box" until 1948 and is seen on 7th July 1959, as class 3F no. 43436 shunts empty stock. The box controlled access to the locomotive depot, the single line eastwards and a short length of double track westwards. (R. C. Riley)

25. A westward view from the box in 1962 includes the staff vegetable allotments and the SR extension to the up platform, complete with concrete fence panels, installed in November 1932. Near the end of it, a pump had earlier been provided to lift water from the River Brue to the works. (E. Wilmshurst)

26. An eastward view shows the road access to the works and in the left distance is the locomotive water tank, with running shed behind it. To the right is the works, most of which had been disused since its closure in 1930. The base of the C & W shop is in the right foreground, the building having burned down in the 1950s. (E. Wilmshurst)

HIGHBRIDGE WORKS

27. The works was designed and built by the SCR and was extended subsequently. Only one locomotive was manufactured but two others were assembled - all three being small saddle tanks. The main task was heavy repairs. No. 70 (formerly 47) was in the erecting shop on 19th August 1928. (H. C. Casserley)

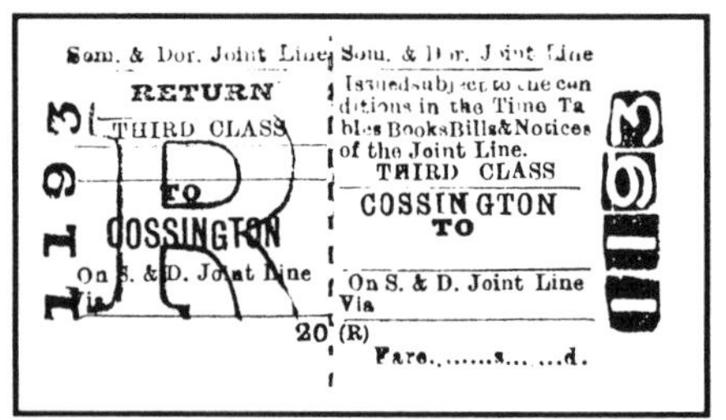

→

29. The MR designed 0-4-4Ts were introduced in 1877 and undertook most passenger work from Highbridge until the 1950s. Behind the sheer legs in this 1935 view is the smith's shop and behind no. 1350 is the mess room. The mark on its end wall was left when the war memorial was removed to the station. The railings in the foreground are round the turntable pit. (H. C. Casserley)

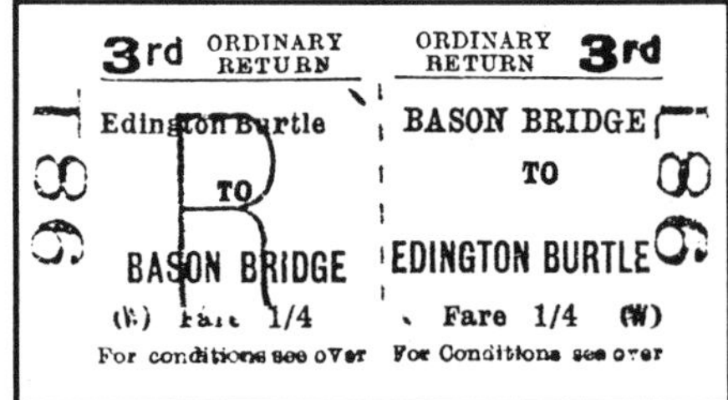

28. On 30th May 1929, the then new no. 23 was facing the boiler shop, the single entrance to the erecting shop being on the left. Gas for lighting the station and works was produced at the railway's own works, near the station approach. (H. C. Casserley)

30. The erecting shop was empty when photographed in 1936 and the unusual locomotive traverser had gone. The horizontal marks on the walls indicate the position of the rails for the gantry crane which was operated by ropes from a small steam engine situated in the far left corner. (H. C. Casserley)

31. At the east of the erecting shop there were three doors leading to short sidings. On the left is the foundry which was added in 1895. In the period 1880 to 1900, the workforce rose from about 350 to 480. The closure in 1930 was catastrophic for the local community. (H. C. Casserley)

HIGHBRIDGE RUNNING SHED

32. The northern part of the works complex was used as a running shed - that part under the roof ventilators. The left hand side was partitioned off and was used as a store. The building on the right of this 1934 picture was part of the paint shop. (D. Cullum coll.)

33. This ex-SDJR locomotive, formerly no 73, was photographed in LMS livery in July 1930, the year in which the beautiful SDJR Prussian blue was discontinued. The coaling equipment seen in this and the previous photograph was similar to that used at Radstock. (H. C. Casserley)

34. The store shed is seen on 20th April 1934 with no. 3158 out of traffic alongside a heap of dry sand for the locomotive sanders. The steel roof trusses of the later building contrast with the timber ones beyond. (H. C. Casserley)

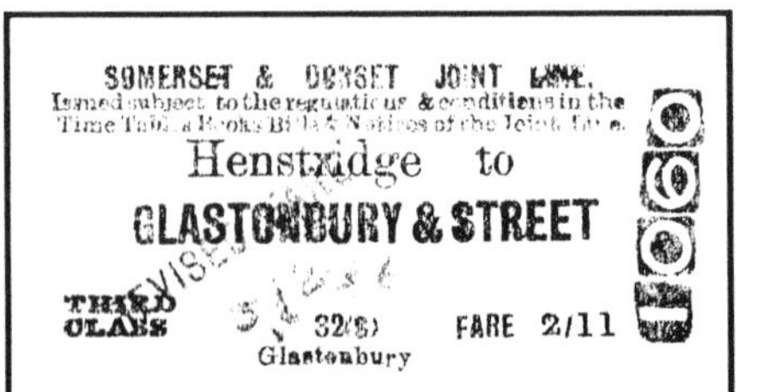

36. BR provided this asbestos shelter for the benefit of staff filling the coal tubs. These were lifted by the hydraulic crane, the jib of which was raised by high pressure water acting upon a vertical piston, which was protected by a gaiter, visible at the top of the column. Unlike its predecessor, it needed the protection of a brazier during frosty weather. Class 3F 0-6-0 no. 43194 was stabled outside for the night of 16th July 1960. (T. Wright)

35. To the left of this view and to the north of the main line, four sidings were added during WWII for US Army traffic. The breakdown train is seen on 4th August 1952. The nearer vehicle was probably built by the SDJR in the 1890s as a five compartment, third class, coach, while the other was older and had two passenger compartments, together with space for the guard and luggage. (J. J. Smith)

37. Pulverised fuel ash is generated in vast quantities in coal fired power stations and is an ideal sub-base for construction of highways on soft ground. In 1970-71, a terminal for the reception of 750,000 tons of this material was constructed on part of the site of Highbridge Works. The flyash was used during the building of the M5 motorway across the level part of Somerset. Part of platform 5 and the old down line is seen on the right, in rain on 23rd April 1971. The line to Bason Bridge was slewed northwards and a ramped track, passing over a discharge bridge, was constructed. The terminal was in use from 27th April until 21st August 1971. The area is now occupied by the Walrow Industrial Estate. (C. Handley)

Diagram to show the revised layout at Highbridge in 1971.

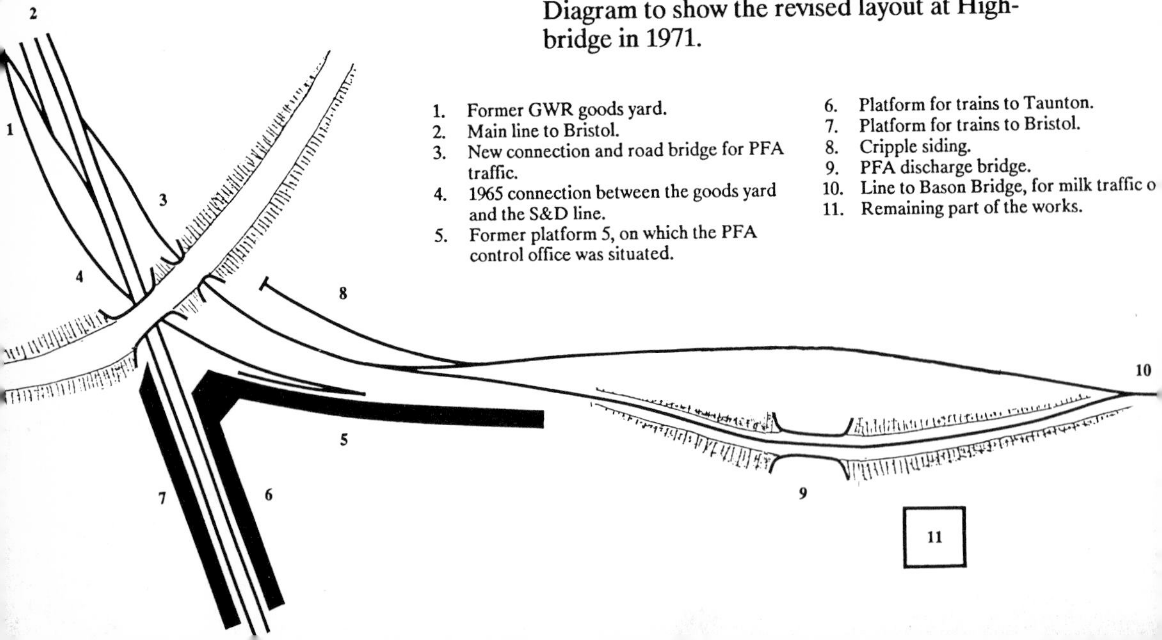

1. Former GWR goods yard.
2. Main line to Bristol.
3. New connection and road bridge for PFA traffic.
4. 1965 connection between the goods yard and the S&D line.
5. Former platform 5, on which the PFA control office was situated.
6. Platform for trains to Taunton.
7. Platform for trains to Bristol.
8. Cripple siding.
9. PFA discharge bridge.
10. Line to Bason Bridge, for milk traffic o
11. Remaining part of the works.

BASON BRIDGE

38. Opened in July 1856, the station had a staff of six in 1928 - From L to R: Freddie Gass (Porter/Shunter), Albert Coombes (Station Master), Cliff Gannicott (Porter/Shunter). Back L to R: Reg Slocombe (Junior Porter), Charlie Jones (Clerk), Edgar Hicks (Clerk). (SDRT coll.)

39. The Wilts United Dairies opened a milk factory adjacent to the railway in 1909 into which sidings were laid. This and the following photographs of Bason Bridge were all taken in the 1960s. (E. Wilmshurst)

40. In earlier years large numbers of milk churns arrived at the platform in vans similar to that behind ex-GWR no. 3201. The station master's house designed in 1901, was squeezed between the railway and the River Brue and is largely obscured by the tree on the left.
(C. L. Caddy)

42. General freight traffic ceased on 10th June 1963 but milk trains continued to run via Highbridge until 2nd October 1972. The milk factory itself closed in 1987, the premises being subsequently used for a variety of industrial purposes ranging from the production of double glazing to dental chairs.
(SDRT/R. Atthill coll.)

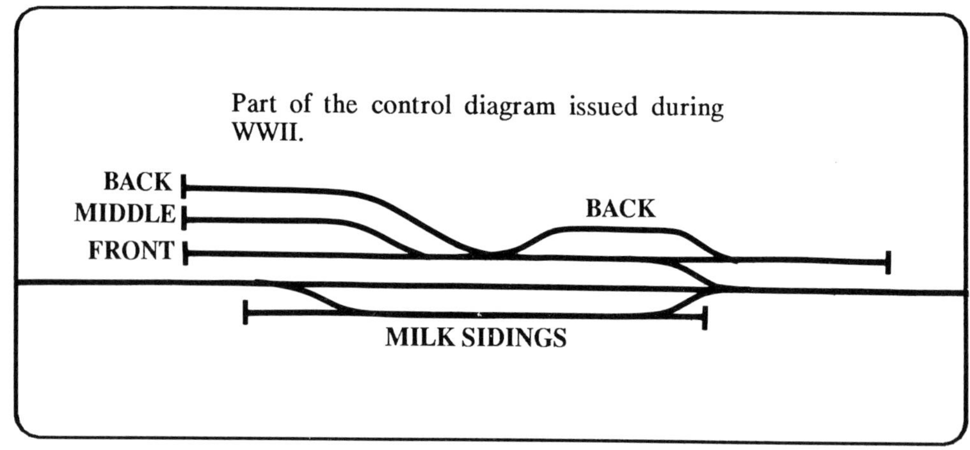

Part of the control diagram issued during WWII.

41. Class 2 2-6-2T no. 41248 was in a filthy condition as it passed the milk factory and a lone fisherman. The revetment is evidence of bank reinforcement, a not uncommon task on the Somerset levels. (T. Wright)

43. The final railtour on the branch ran from Waterloo via Bournemouth and returned via Bristol, Bath (Green Park), Templecombe and Salisbury, on 6th March 1966. Nos. 41283 and 41249 pass Huntspill Crossing cottage, where the drinking water cans stood by the gate. (J. J. Smith)

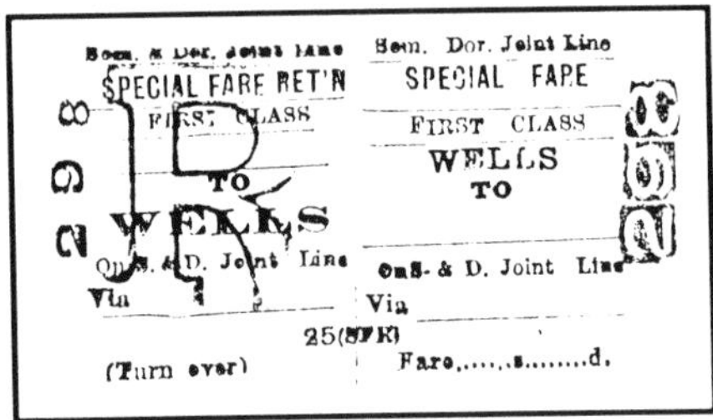

Som. & Dor. Joint Line
SPECIAL FARE RET'N
FIRST CLASS
TO
WELLS
On S. & D. Joint Line
Via
(Turn over)

298

Som. Dor. Joint Line
SPECIAL FARE
FIRST CLASS
WELLS
TO
On S. & D. Joint Line
Via
Fare......s........d.

298

25(S&R)

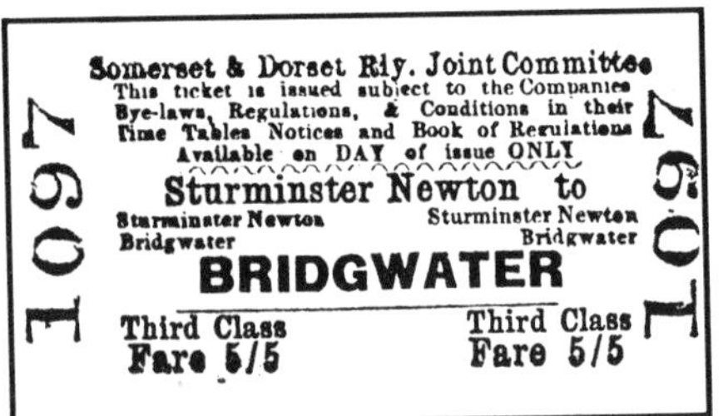

1097

Somerset & Dorset Rly. Joint Committee
This ticket is issued subject to the Companies Bye-laws, Regulations, & Conditions in their Time Tables Notices and Book of Regulations
Available on DAY of issue ONLY
Sturminster Newton to

Sturminster Newton	Sturminster Newton
Bridgwater	Bridgwater

BRIDGWATER

Third Class	Third Class
Fare 5/5	Fare 5/5

1097

→

45. The Bridgwater branch departure at 10.50am on 4th August 1952 was hauled by ex-LMS no. 1379, which was of Midland Railway origin. Wild flowers in the track added to the rural charm, while the large condensing pipe on the 0-4-4T was a legacy of the days it worked underground in London. (J. J. Smith)

EDINGTON BURTLE

44. Opened as Edington Road in 1856, the first station had a single platform on the south side of the line and no sidings. The opening of the branch to Bridgwater on 21st July 1890 resulted in the name being changed to Edington Junction. A train from Bridgwater is seen approaching the bay platform. The vans on the left are standing in the adjacent siding. (Mowat coll.)

46. Seen from a train from Highbridge on 5th September 1952, 0-6-0 no. 43194 (formerly SDJR no. 62) waits on the foot crossing, while the incoming tablet is collected on its footplate. The bay starting signals and part of the cattle dock are visible. (H. C. Casserley)

The layout marked on the 1904 map changed little until 1956. Two sidings had been added in 1899 to cope with the traffic then emanating from the branch.

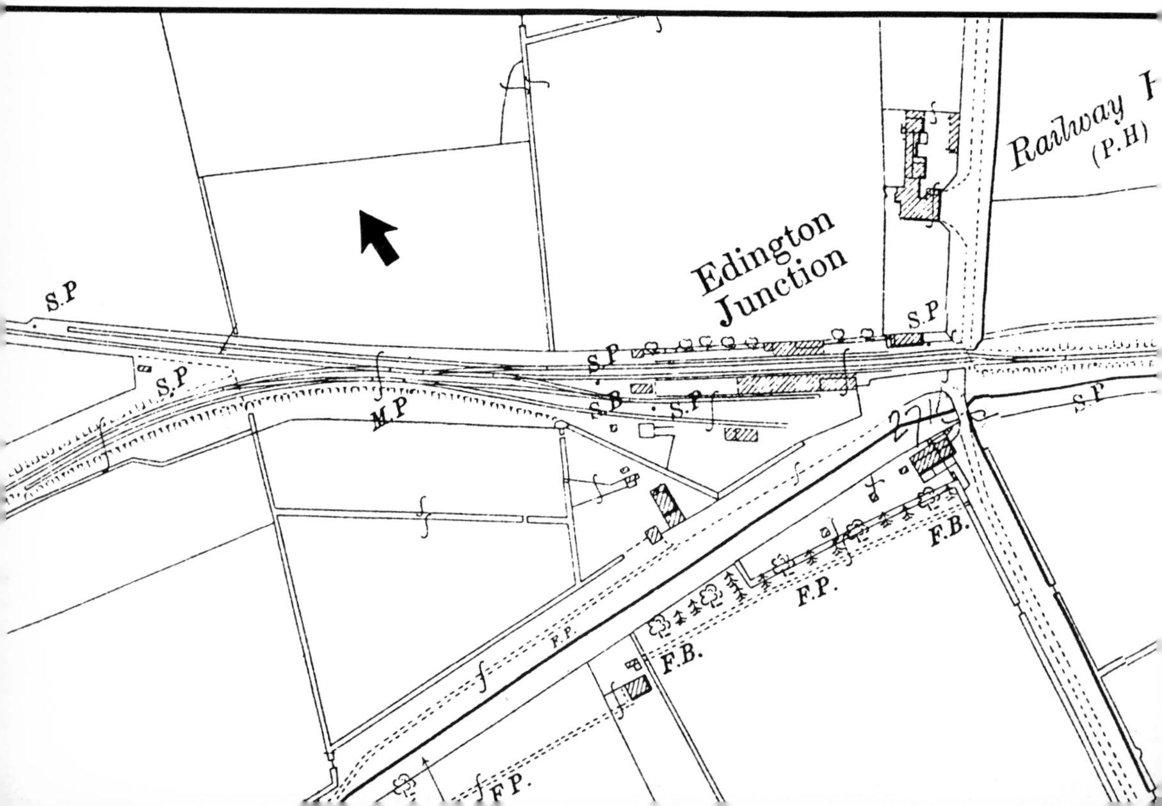

Railway H
(P.H)
Edington Junction
S.P
S.P
S.P
S.P
S.P
S.P
M.P
S.B
F.B.
F.P.
F.P.
F.B.
F.P.

47. The 6.49pm from Evercreech Junction on 15th July 1960 was departing behind no. 43194, which in SDJR days was much cleaner and bore the number 62. Passenger services to Bridgwater ceased on 1st December 1952 and the station was renamed Edington Burtle on 8th June 1953. (T. Wright)

48. By August 1963, nature was trying hard to decorate the little used remaining platform. On 4th February 1956, the signal box had been closed and the loop and all sidings except one were taken out of use. (C. L. Caddy)

49. The siding that was kept was apparently relaid and made a direct connection to the single running line. Goods facilities were retained until 13th July 1964, but the goods shed which once stood to the right of the van disappeared much earlier. (E. Wilmshurst)

lower left

50. After the loss of the 39-lever signal box in 1956, ground frames were provided for the siding and the level crossing control, both being just out of view in this 1964 picture. (C. L. Caddy)

51. Only the birdsong and aroma of the hedgerow are needed to complete this sylvan scene in the summer of 1965, sadly the last summer of operation. The station was situated half a mile south of Edington Burtle and two miles north of Edington, the combined population of which was about 300 for much of the life of the line. (R. M. Casserley)

52. Class 2 2-6-2T no. 41296 drifts in with the last 2.18pm from Highbridge on Saturday 1st January 1966, the planned closure day. The death pains lasted until 6th March. Water was carried in cans to the end. (E. Wilmshurst)

53. The station house (to the right of the crossing) still stands, as does the Railway Hotel (extreme right) but this has been renamed *Tom Mogg*, in memory of a long serving porter/signalman at the station. On the left is the disused Glastonbury Canal.
(E. Wilmshurst)

Bridgwater Branch

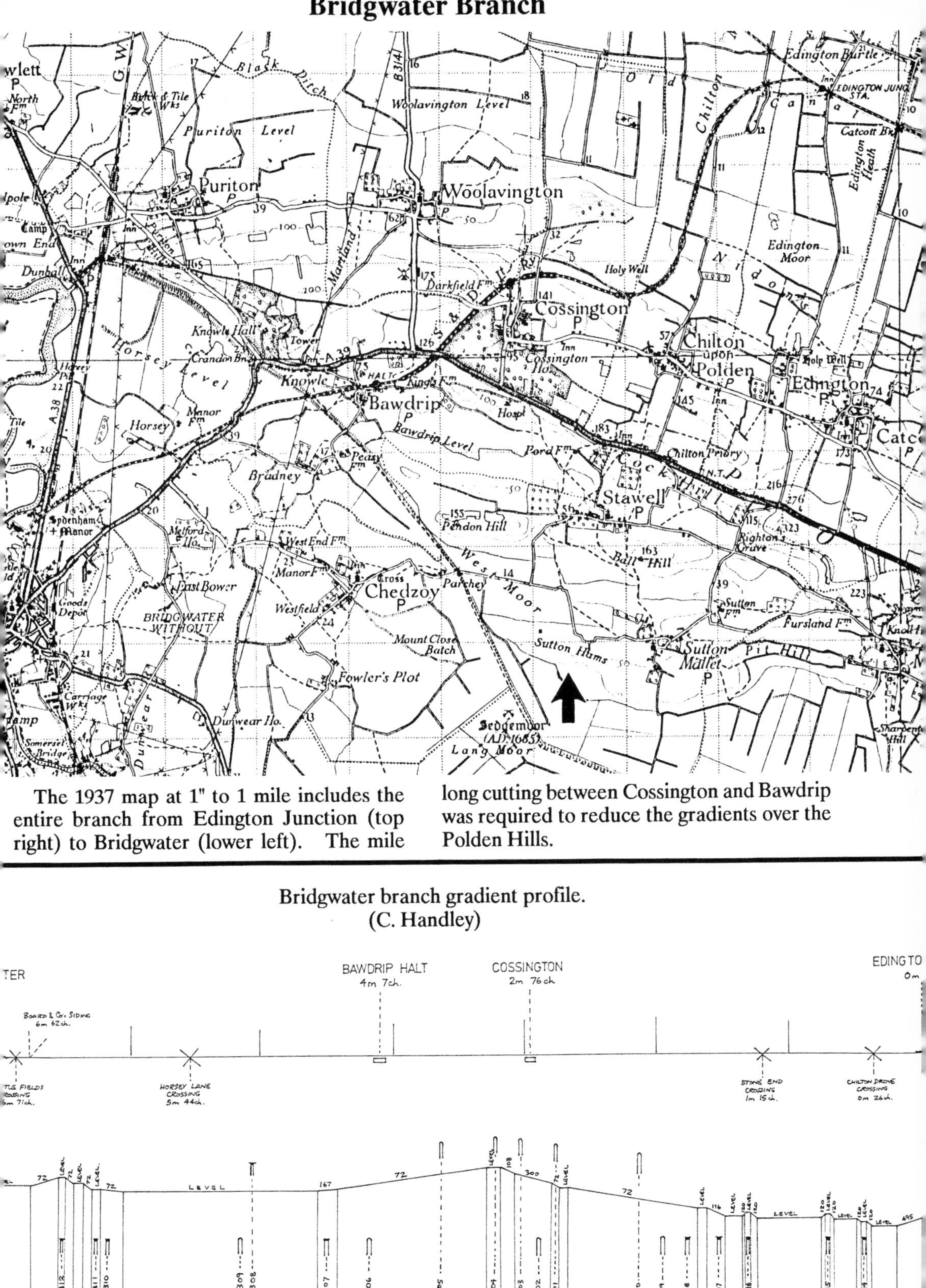

The 1937 map at 1" to 1 mile includes the entire branch from Edington Junction (top right) to Bridgwater (lower left). The mile long cutting between Cossington and Bawdrip was required to reduce the gradients over the Polden Hills.

Bridgwater branch gradient profile.
(C. Handley)

COSSINGTON

54. Originally the only intermediate station on the branch, it was well situated in relation to the village. The hut on the right housed the ground frame which controlled access to the goods siding, which remained in use until 4th October 1954. The hut was later moved to the East Somerset Railway. A mile to the east, another siding served Board's Quarry, on the south side of the line, until 1933. (Lens of Sutton)

56. The grey limestone building ceased to be used by passengers on 1st December 1952 and is seen to be in good condition in 1958. Cossington is one of a string of villages set on the spring line of the northern slope of the Polden Hills and was the only one to have a station close to it. (R. M. Casserley)

The 1902 map marks five cattle pens, which were well used on Bridgwater market days. Until 1895, the track layout necessitated cattle being taken via Edington Junction, a source of annoyance to stockholders and animals alike.

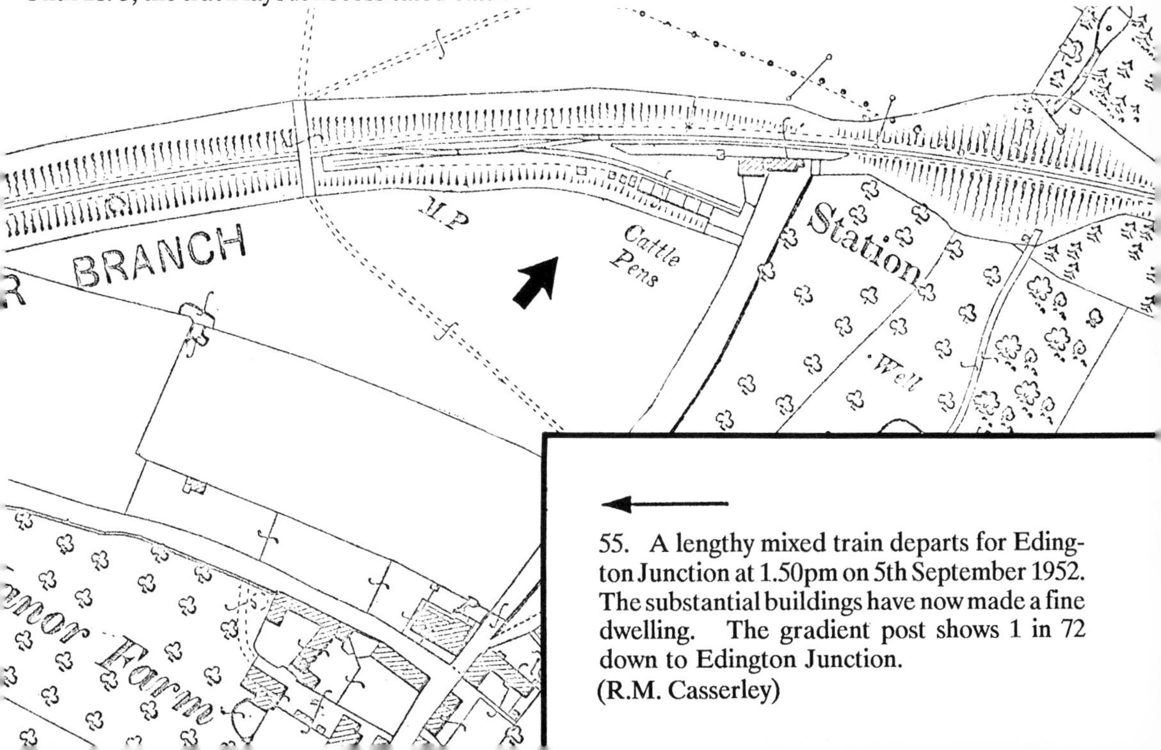

55. A lengthy mixed train departs for Edington Junction at 1.50pm on 5th September 1952. The substantial buildings have now made a fine dwelling. The gradient post shows 1 in 72 down to Edington Junction.
(R.M. Casserley)

BAWDRIP HALT

57. Although the railway passed close to the centre of the village, no stopping place was provided until 7th July 1923, a surprising omission. A shelter was added in the following year and over 200 passengers per week were recorded. (Lens of Sutton)

The 1930 edition shows the proximity of the halt to the village. Part of the track bed is now occupied by a bungalow, aptly named *Essandee.*

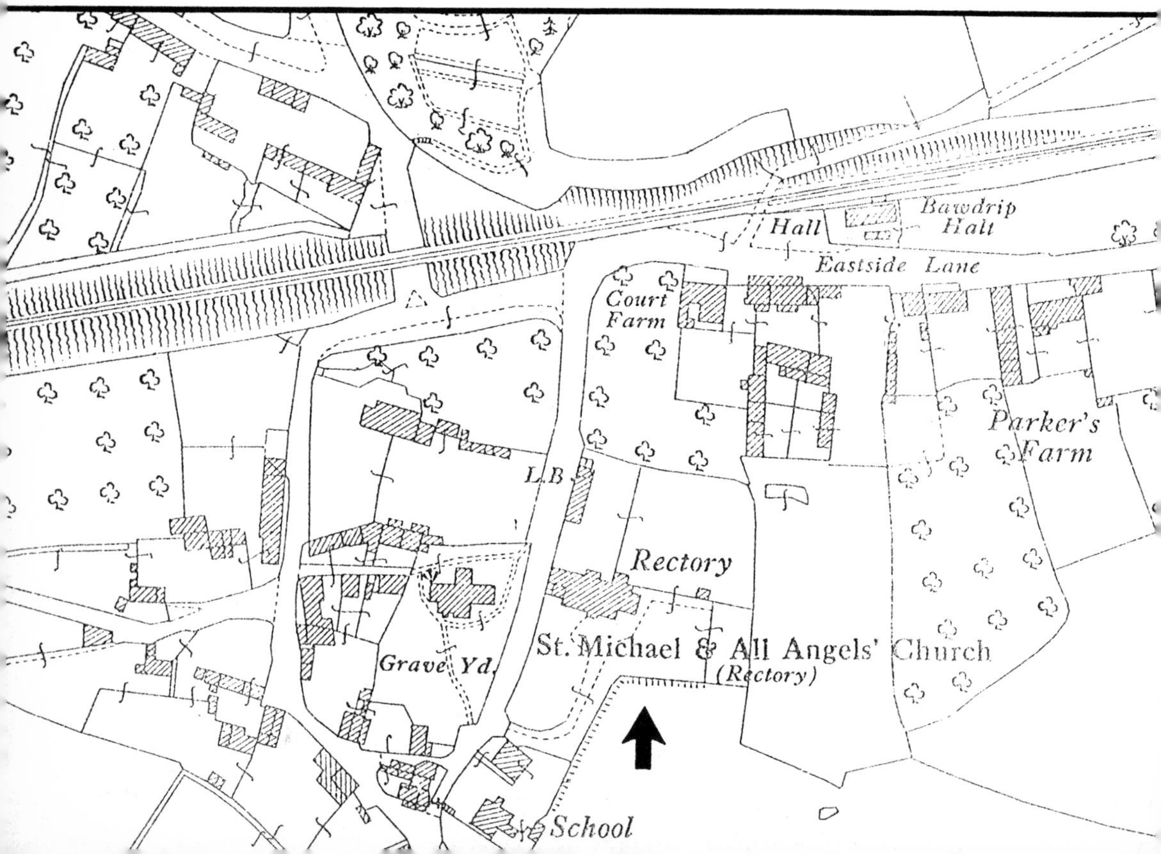

BRIDGWATER NORTH

For many centuries, the port of Bridgwater was regarded as the most important between Bristol and Barnstaple. In consequence, the town's industries developed and the fine Georgian buildings of Castle Street reflect the resulting wealth. The docks were built around 1840 and remained in use until 1970. Bridgwater's products have included bricks, tiles, pottery, "Bath Brick" for cleaning (from river bank slime) glazed pipes (to 1900), flower pots, timber milling, and wicker work. There has also been rope making, ship building, foundry work, cellophane (from 1938) and light industries in profusion.

58. A blurred but interesting picture taken from a train arriving in the 1930s shows the approach to the goods yard and locomotive shed. An extra siding and a 5-ton crane had been added in 1899. The town had a population of nearly 15,000 when the line opened and so was a good source of traffic. (Mowat coll.)

59. The station was entirely different from any other on the S&D system, having been built by the independent Bridgwater Railway. The generous canopy remained until the end of passenger services and is seen, along with the spacious goods shed, in August 1952. The suffix "North" was added on 26th September 1949. (J. J. Smith)

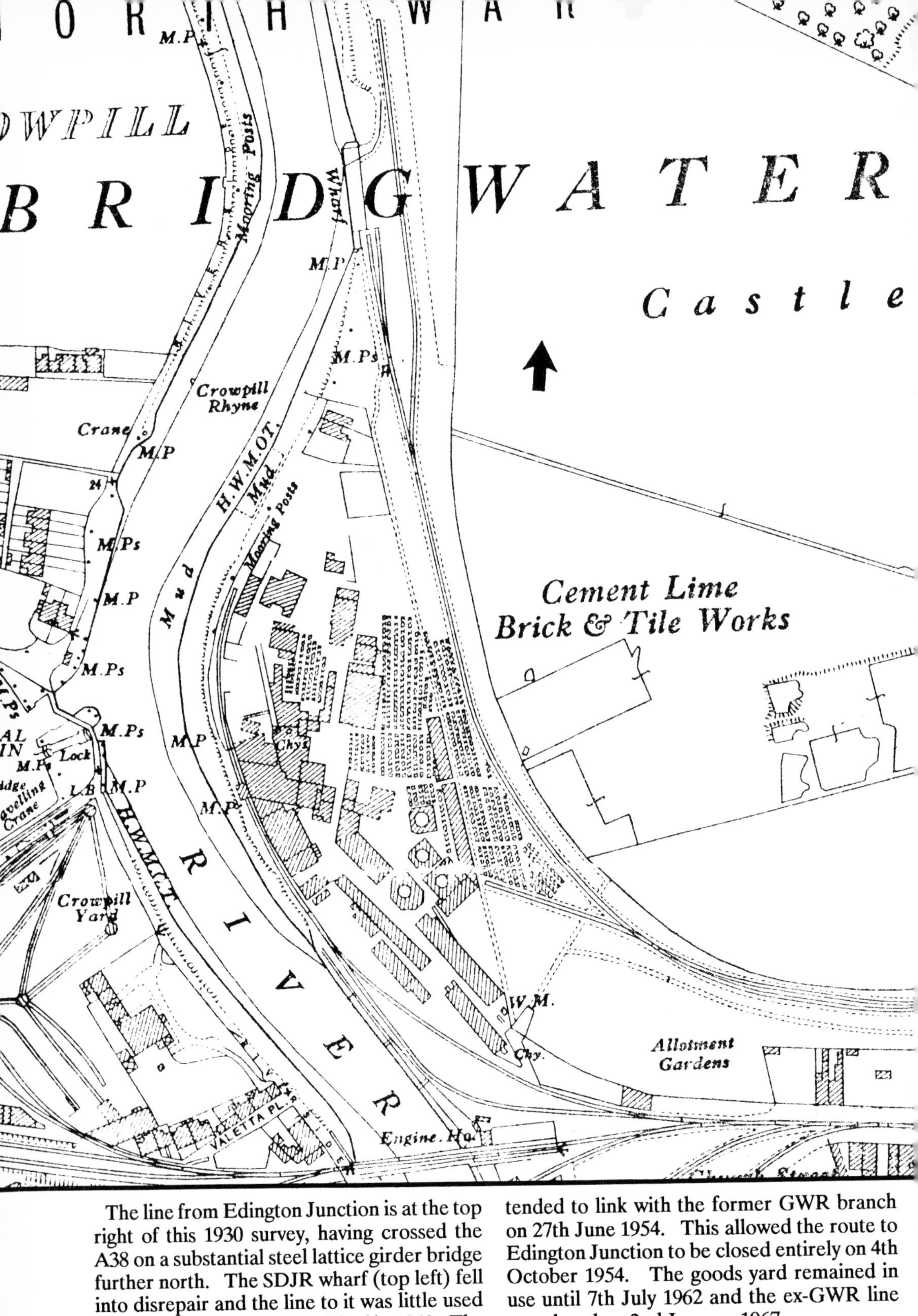

The line from Edington Junction is at the top right of this 1930 survey, having crossed the A38 on a substantial steel lattice girder bridge further north. The SDJR wharf (top left) fell into disrepair and the line to it was little used after 1909, being eventually lifted in 1942. The siding to the right of the cattle pens was extended to link with the former GWR branch on 27th June 1954. This allowed the route to Edington Junction to be closed entirely on 4th October 1954. The goods yard remained in use until 7th July 1962 and the ex-GWR line was closed on 2nd January 1967.

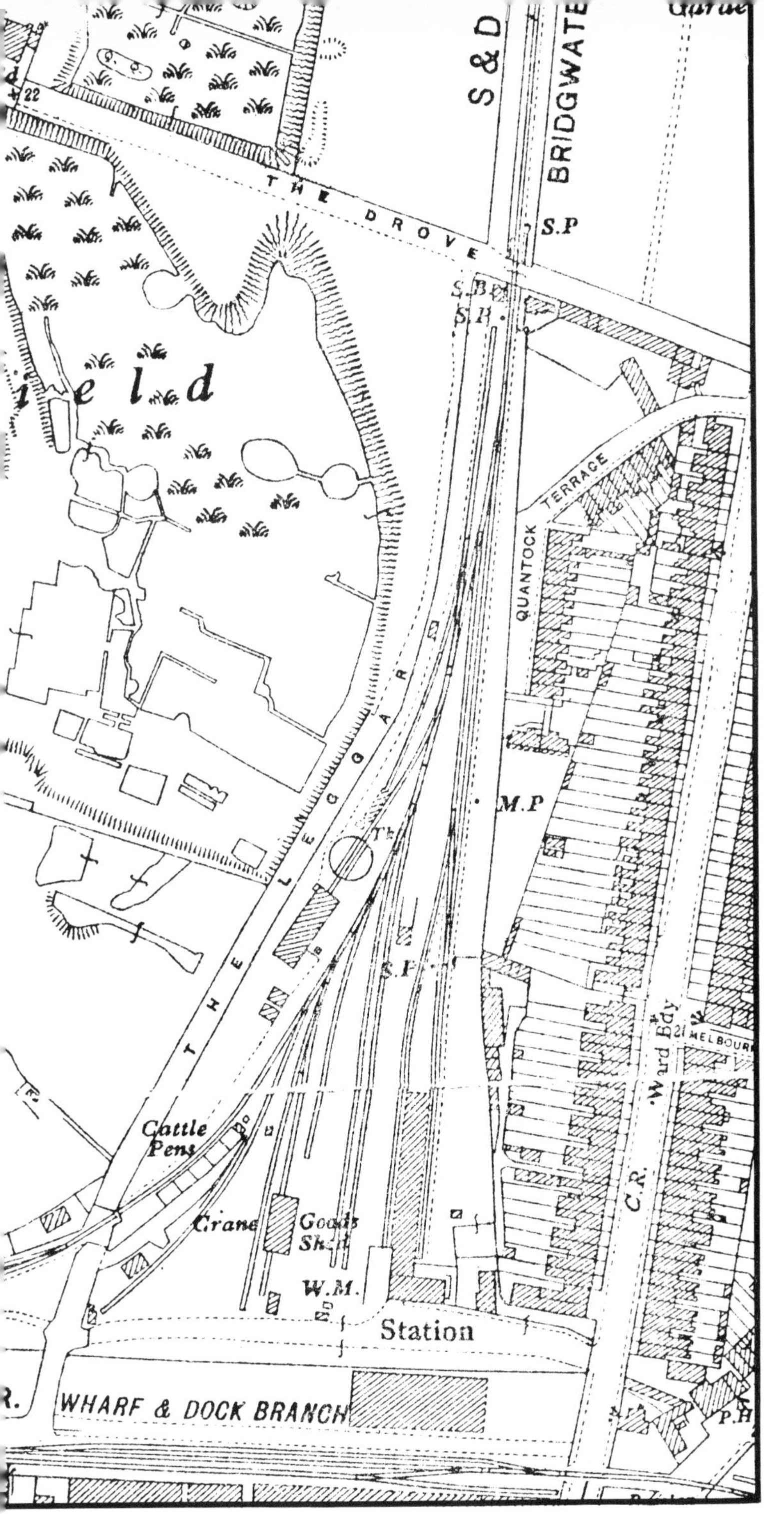

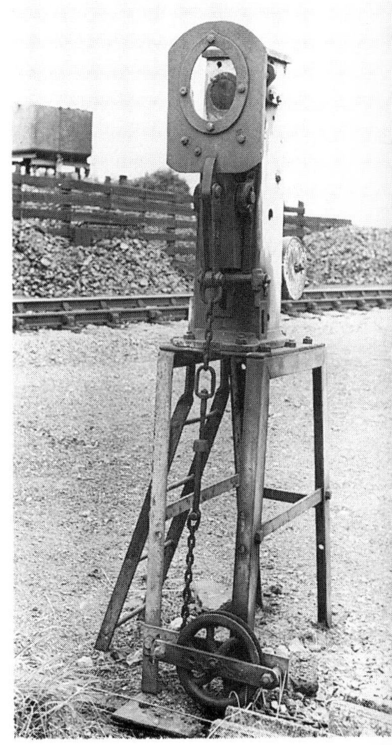

60. The ground signal in the foreground of the previous picture is shown in more detail. An indication to proceed was given when the red plate tilted forward to a horizontal position. A Steven's throw-face shunt signal of this type is included amongst the SDRT's exhibits at Washford. (J. J. Smith)

1924

BRIDGWATER and EDINGTON.—Southern.

Miles	Down.	Week Days only. mrn	mrn	mrn	mrn	a	aft	aft	aft	aft	aft	
—	Bridgwater ....dep.	6 35	9 30	1035	1120	1 10	3 10	5 10	6 30	8 20	9 35	....
—	Bawdrip Halt	....	9 36	1041	1126	1 17	3 16	5 16	6 36	8 26	9 41	....
4½	Cossington..................	6 43	9 40	1045	1130	1 21	3 20	5 20	6 40	8 30	9 45	....
7	Edington Jun. ....arr.	6 49	9 46	1051	1136	1 27	3 26	5 26	6 46	8 36	9 51	....

Miles	Up.	Week Days only. mrn	mrn		mrn	mrn	aft	a	aft	aft	aft	aft	aft
—	Edington Junction ....dep.	8 2	9 0	Weds.	9 55	1058	1 35	1220	4 20	5 36	7 22	9 0	10 2
2¾	Cossington	8 9	9 7		10 2	11 5	1 42	1227	4 27	5 43	7 29	9 7	10 9
—	Bawdrip Halt..............	8 13	9 11		10 6	11 9	1 46	1231	4 31	5 47	7 33	9 12	1014
7	Bridgwater ‡ ..arr.	8 13	9 16		1011	1114	1 51	1236	4 36	5 52	7 38	9 17	1019

a Mondays, Thursdays, and Saturdays. ‡ Station for Spaxton; nearly ¼ mile to G.W. Station.

61. The engine shed was lengthened in 1898 to accommodate the two engines required by then to work the seven mile long branch. In 1922, it was decided that the line could be worked by an engine from Templecombe and so the shed remained empty until 1928, when it was leased to the Co-op for use as a store. On 4th August 1952 ex-MR no. 58072 was photographed close to the 50ft turntable which remained serviceable until the end. (J. J. Smith)

62. Push-pull working commenced in 1928 and most trains were so worked thereafter, although there were usually one or two mixed trains each day. No. 58072 prepares to leave on 5th September 1952 and will probably collect the wagons from the adjacent platform. (H. C. Casserley)

63. The same engine is seen on the same day with the 17-lever signal box and The Drove level crossing in the distance. The gates were worked by hand. The entire area is now occupied by industrial premises. 200 yds beyond the crossing, Board's siding diverged to the left to their cement works. For many years railway revenue was derived from the transport of raw materials from the quarry beyond Cossington. (H. C. Casserley)

64. The round-headed windows gave the impression that this was a LSWR station. It remained standing until 1984, when it was demolished to make way for a Sainsbury's store which opened in 1989. The station master's house is on the right. (Lens of Sutton)

SHAPWICK

65. The station opened with the line and the excessive "six-foot" between the tracks was a lasting reminder of its broad gauge past. The building on the right was a replacement for one burned down on 25th September 1900. Beyond it is a private goods shed, the nearest building on the right being the tariff shed, used for public parcel traffic. (Mowat coll.)

The 1902 map shows just one siding at the east end of the yard, a second one being added later to handle the traffic in peat, from the nearby producers.

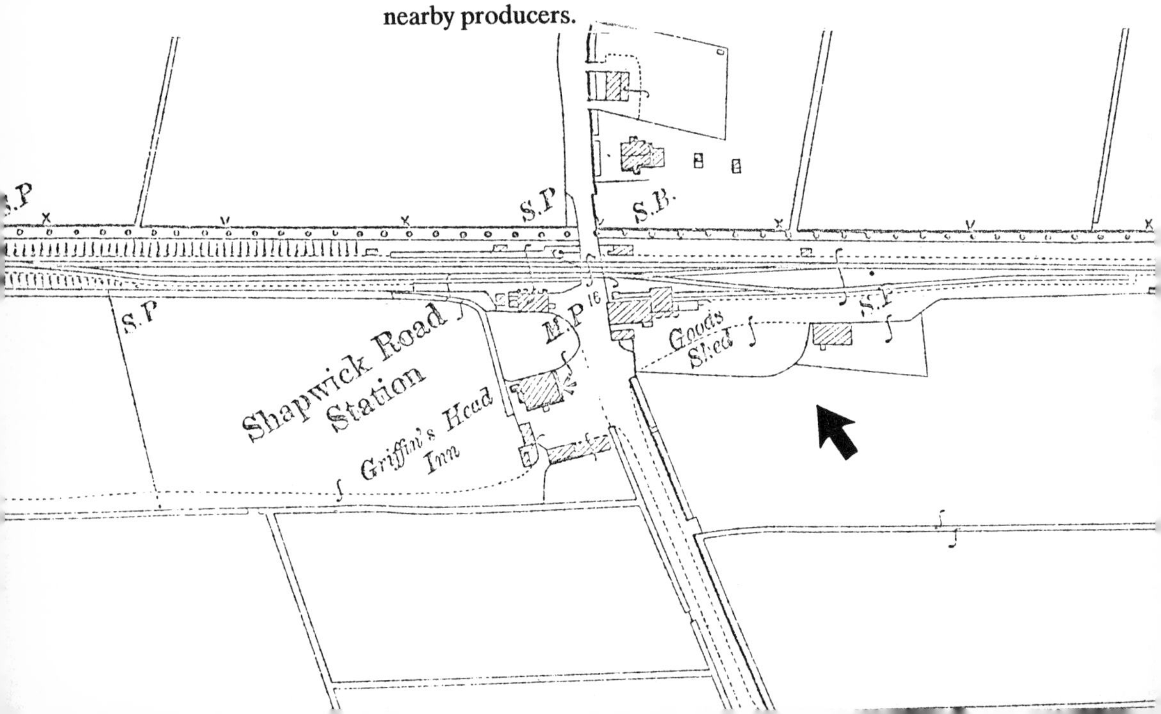

66. The 1901 signal box, seen in August 1963, remained in use as a block post controlling the passing loop until the line closed. The small goods yard, partly visible on the right, ceased to receive traffic on 10th June 1963. (C. L. Caddy)

67. The original timber and earth platforms were replaced by SR "harps and slabs" but oil lighting was retained. The station was over two miles north of Shapwick and a mile south of Westhay, surrounded by wetlands. (C. L. Caddy)

68. A view from the 17-lever signal box in January 1966 emphasises the station's desolate location. Apart from the goods yard gate, there is now no trace of railway property and peace reigns on the nearby Nature Conservancy's Shapwick Heath. The nameboard is preserved by the SDRT at Washford. (E. Wilmshurst)

69. One and a quarter miles east of Shapwick the Eclipse Peat Co. had a siding on the north side of the line, facing Ashcott. To the west of it, their 2 ft. gauge railway crossed the main line on the level, at an occupation crossing devoid of signals. The 1922 agreement for the crossing was for its use by horse and cart but the little railway appeared in about 1930, without any record in head office. (S. C. Nash)

70. On 19th August 1949, the 8.0 am mixed train from Glastonbury to Bridgwater, hauled by 0-6-0 no. 3260 (ex-SDJR no. 76), collided with the Eclipse Peat Co's petrol engine, which had stalled on the crossing. Its driver had run along the track to give warning but was not seen owing to fog. The Bath (Green Park) crane travelled via Bristol to rerail the coach but the locomotive was cut up into 4-ton pieces during the autumn of 1949. Twelve months later whistle boards and telephones were installed. (SDRT/R. Atthill coll.)

71. The Eclipse Peat Co's narrow gauge line crosses the main line and South Drain in the foreground, while their works and private siding is in the background. We are looking towards Ashcott. (C. G. Maggs)

ASHCOTT

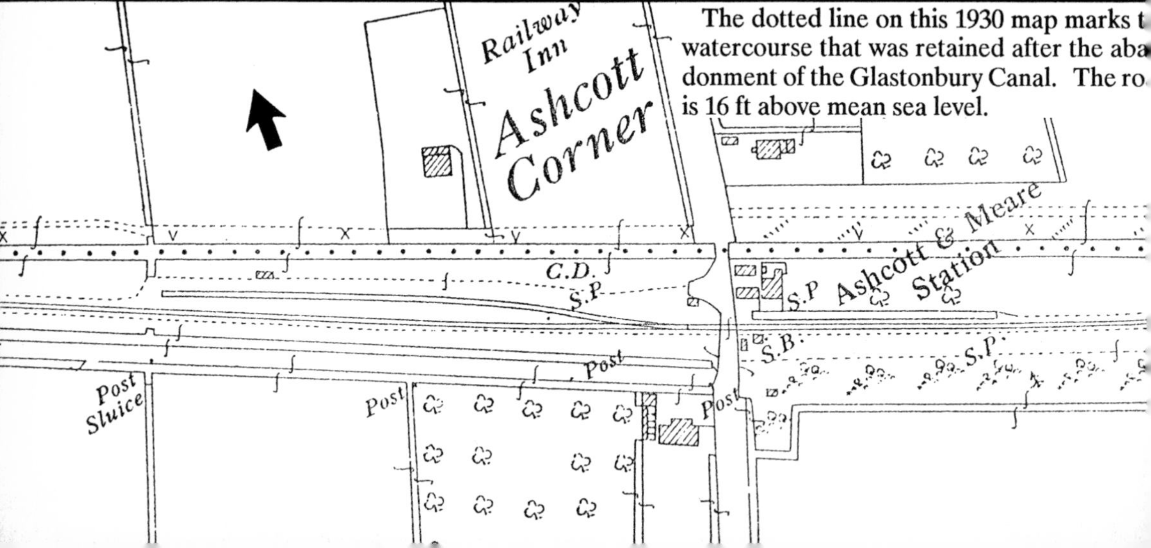

The dotted line on this 1930 map marks t
watercourse that was retained after the aba
donment of the Glastonbury Canal. The ro
is 16 ft above mean sea level.

72. The small station opened with the line and was on the east side of the lane that linked the villages of Ashcott (two miles to the south) with Meare (one mile to the north). This view towards Glastonbury shows the waiting room and booking office on the extreme left. (Lens of Sutton)

74. The siding is seen a month after its closure on 13th July 1964, the points having been operated from the ground frame adjacent to the gates. (C. L. Caddy)

73. The solitary siding was west of the road, the loading gauge being visible in the distance in this 1932 view. As at Shapwick, the main traffic was peat. (Mowat coll.)

75. The earlier timber platform had been replaced by a SR concrete structure part of which was still standing, along with the station house, in 1989. Nearly one mile to the east the Petfu peat sidings had been brought into use in 1920, on the north side of the line. (C. L. Caddy)

GLASTONBURY AND STREET

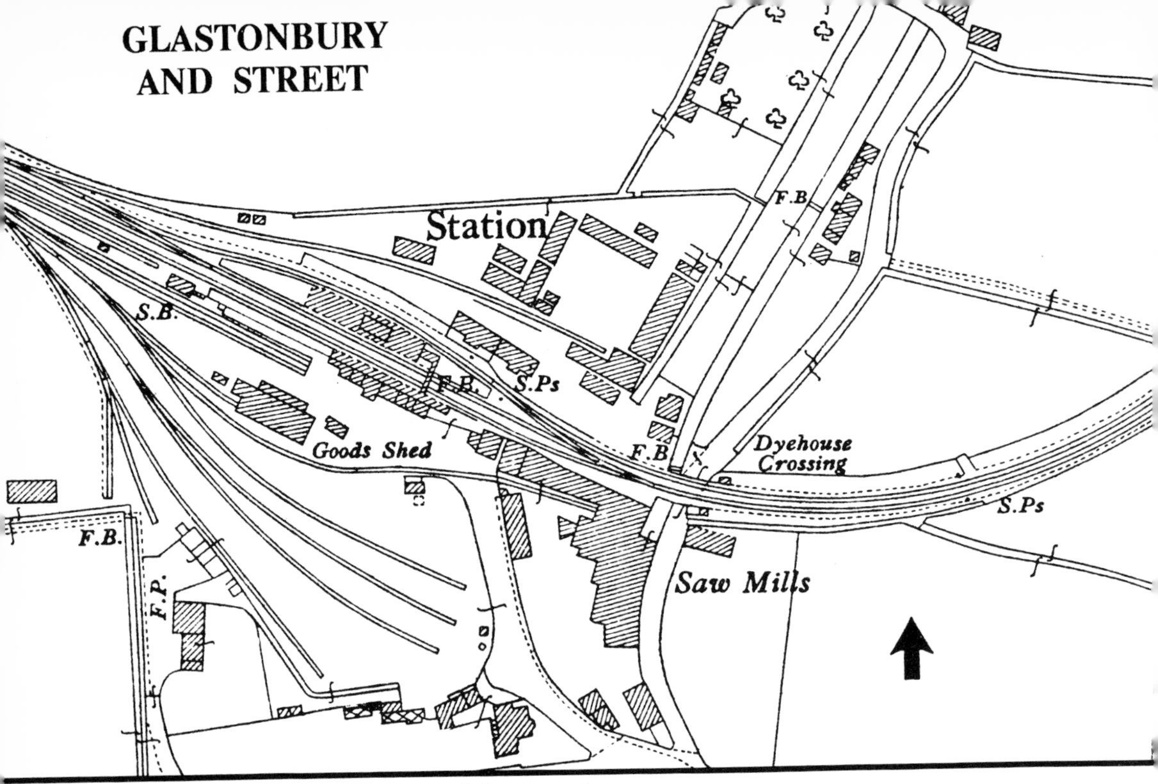

The 1930 survey includes part of the curved track which comprised two single lines, one to Wells and the other to Evercreech Junction. F. B. refers to footbridges which passed over a stream which ran under the railway, adajacent to the level crossing, and then under Snow's sawmill.

76. Flooding was a frequent problem and was a reminder of the proximity of the station to the former canal basin. An interesting feature of this photograph is the wicker basket for the safe transit of mailbags. (Lens of Sutton)

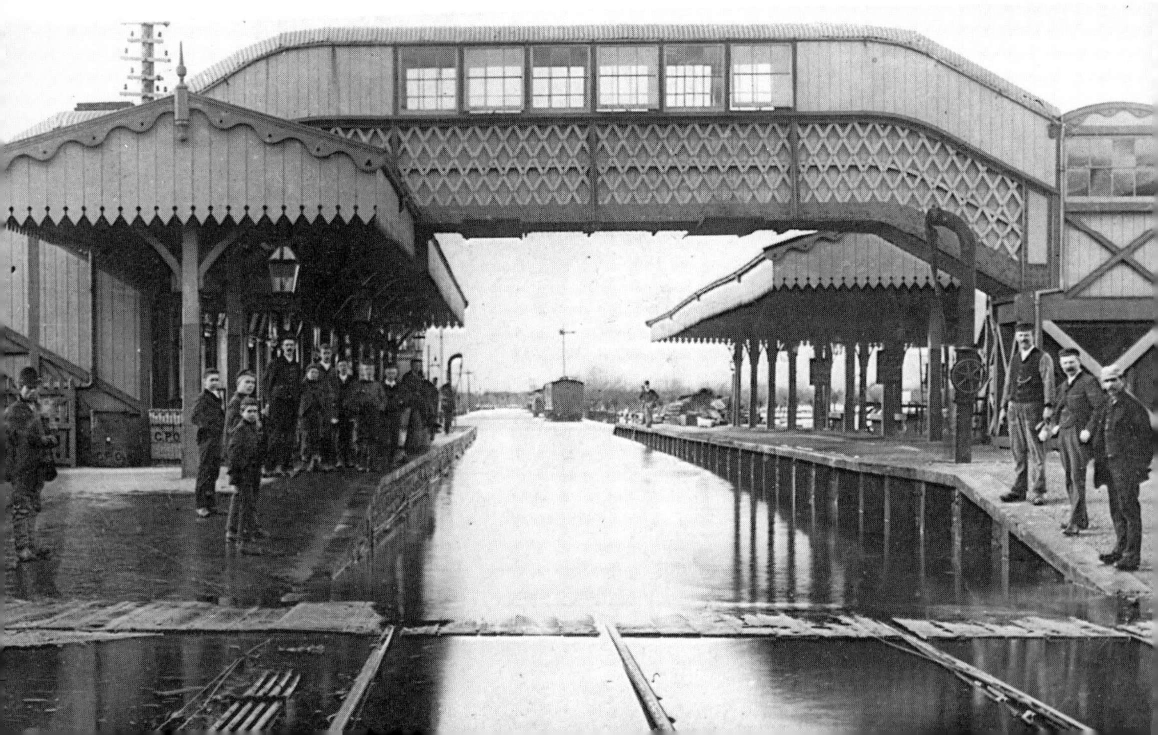

77. Behind the GNR wagon is the oil store, which was, at most stations, usually remote from other buildings for safety reasons. The locomotive appears to be no. 25 and its train includes sheeted wagons, probably containing hay. (J. C. Locke/R. C. Riley coll.)

78. The suffix was added in 1886, Street being an almost equally populous area two miles south of the town. Although of Roman origin, Street developed greatly during the railway era as a result of the improved transport for its main product - shoes. The signal box once had 24 levers and three tablet machines.
(D. Cullum)

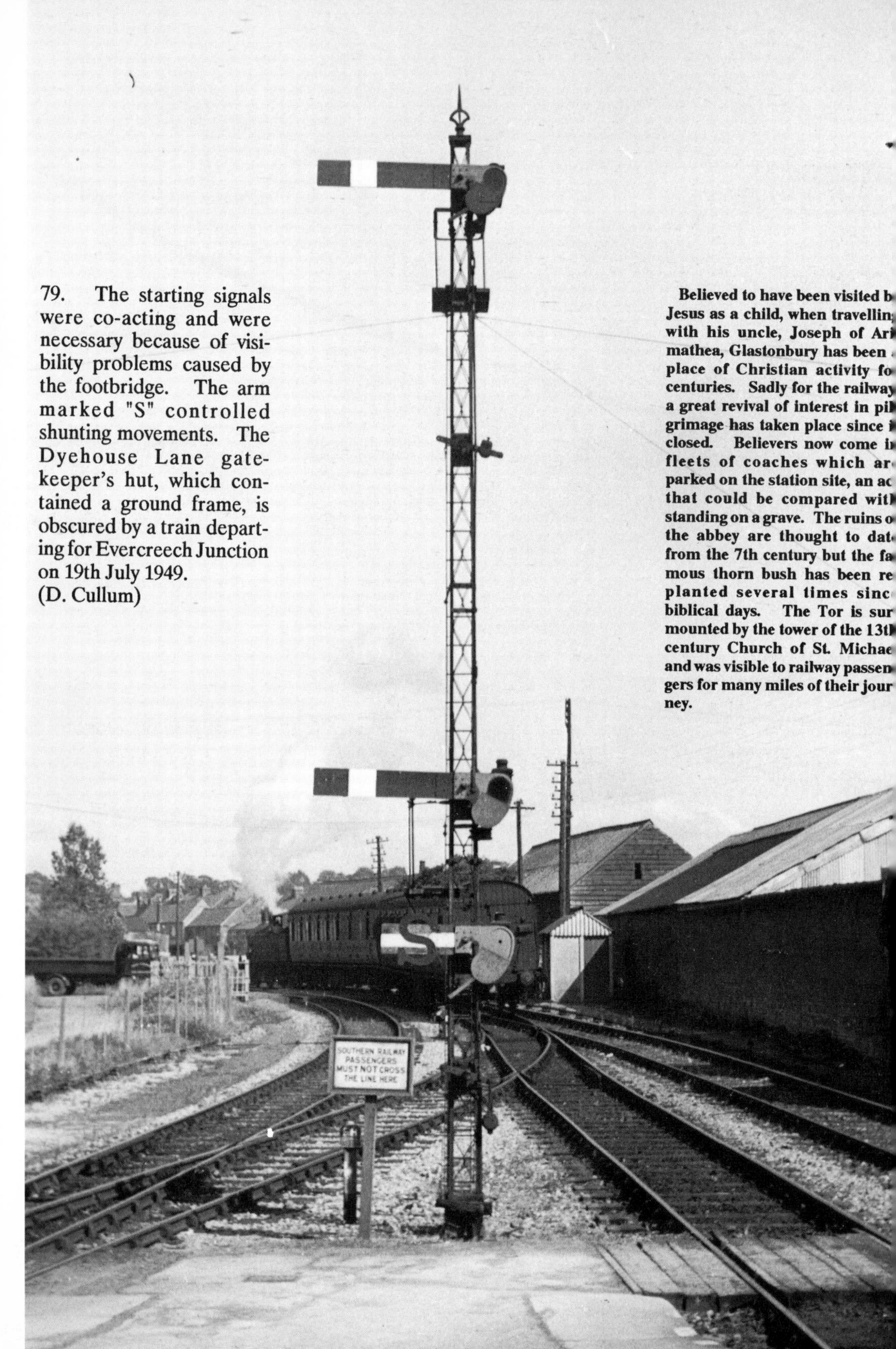

79. The starting signals were co-acting and were necessary because of visibility problems caused by the footbridge. The arm marked "S" controlled shunting movements. The Dyehouse Lane gatekeeper's hut, which contained a ground frame, is obscured by a train departing for Evercreech Junction on 19th July 1949.
(D. Cullum)

Believed to have been visited b Jesus as a child, when travellin with his uncle, Joseph of Ari mathea, Glastonbury has been place of Christian activity fo centuries. Sadly for the railway a great revival of interest in pil grimage has taken place since i closed. Believers now come i fleets of coaches which ar parked on the station site, an ac that could be compared wit standing on a grave. The ruins o the abbey are thought to dat from the 7th century but the fa mous thorn bush has been re planted several times sinc biblical days. The Tor is sur mounted by the tower of the 13t century Church of St. Michae and was visible to railway passen gers for many miles of their jour ney.

80. A busy period was recorded on 2nd October 1951. On the left is the 9.10am from Templecombe which arrived at 10.23 and would leave at 10.32; centre is the 9.45 from Burnham-on-Sea (arr. 10.26, dep. 10.28) and on the right is the 10.40 departure for Wells. The locomotives are ex-MR 0-4-4Ts nos. 58088 and 58046. The box probably contains fresh fish, a regular commodity on passenger trains which gave rise to a distinctive smell that lingered in guards vans. (S. C. Nash)

81. Boxes of Clark's shoes formed a major part of goods outward. This photograph from 16th July 1960 features the 5.20pm milk train from Bason Bridge, headed by class 3F no. 43593, and the fully glazed footbridge, which was intact until closure. (T. Wright)

83. Class 2 2-6-2T no. 41290, one van and a coach form the 1.15pm Evercreech Junction to Highbridge on 1st January 1966 and are seen from the signal box steps. Also visible is Glastonbury Tor, St. John's Church and some of the buildings of the engineer's yard. The yard area was used as a US Army transit camp during WWII and the buildings have more recently been adapted as homes and business premises. (S. C. Nash)

82. The station flower beds were still in good order when recorded in August 1964 and parcels abound. The saw mills on the left had their own private siding, a section of which was still in situ in 1989. The entire site was levelled in 1984 but the island platform canopy was rebuilt in one of the town's car parks to cover an open air market. (C. L. Caddy)

1906

GLASTONBURY and WELLS.—Somerset and Dorset.

Miles.	Week Days.	mrn	mrn	mrn	aft	aft	aft	aft	aft	aft	aft	aft								
	98 Bridgwater........dep.	6 50	8 50	10 0	12 5	....	3 35	....	5 30	....	8 20	....	...	...	...	...	...	...	...	...
	Glastonbury and Street dep.	8 15	9 35	11 0	1 0	2 40	4 17	5 35	6 15	7 25	9 0	9 45	...	...	...	...	...	...	...	...
3	Polsham..................	8 26	9 44	11 9	1 8	2 48	4 25	5 41	6 22	7 34	9 8	9 53	...	...	...	...	...	...	...	...
5½	Wells ** 40............arr.	8 33	9 49	1114	1 13	2 53	4 30	5 46	6 27	7 39	9 13	9 58	...	...	...	...	...	...	...	...
Miles.	Week Days. Priory Road Station,	mrn	mrn	mrn	aft	aft	aft	aft	aft	aft	aft	aft								
	Wells....................dep.	7 15	9 10	1015	1225	2 15	3 55	5 5	5 55	6 40	8 0	9 25	...	...	...	...	...	...	...	...
2½	Polsham.............[98, 99	7 21	9 16	1020	1230	2 20	4 0	5 12	6 1	6 47	8 7	9 30	...	...	...	...	...	...	...	...
5½	Glastonbury and Street arr.	7 27	9 22	1026	1236	2 26	4 6	5 18	6 6	6 57	8 13	9 36	...	...	...	...	...	...	...	...
19½	99 Bridgwater........arr.	8 7	....	1128	1 20	3 5	....	6 7	....	....	8 52	1014	...	...	...	...	...	...	...	...

** Priory Road; about ¼ mile to Great Western Station.

84. This fine building still stands at the end of the station approach and originally housed the SCR offices and the Railway Inn. It ceased to be used for railway purposes in 1877 and is now the administrative offices for nearby Snow's timber yard. This is the north elevation in 1968. (S. W. Baker)

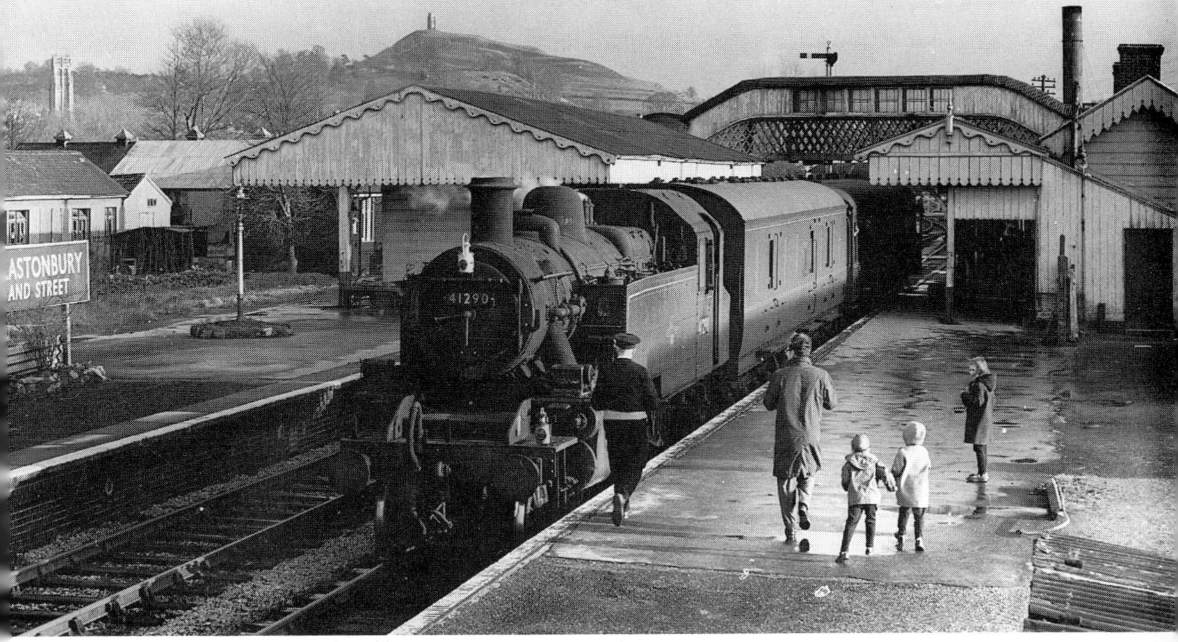
ASTONBURY
AND STREET
41290

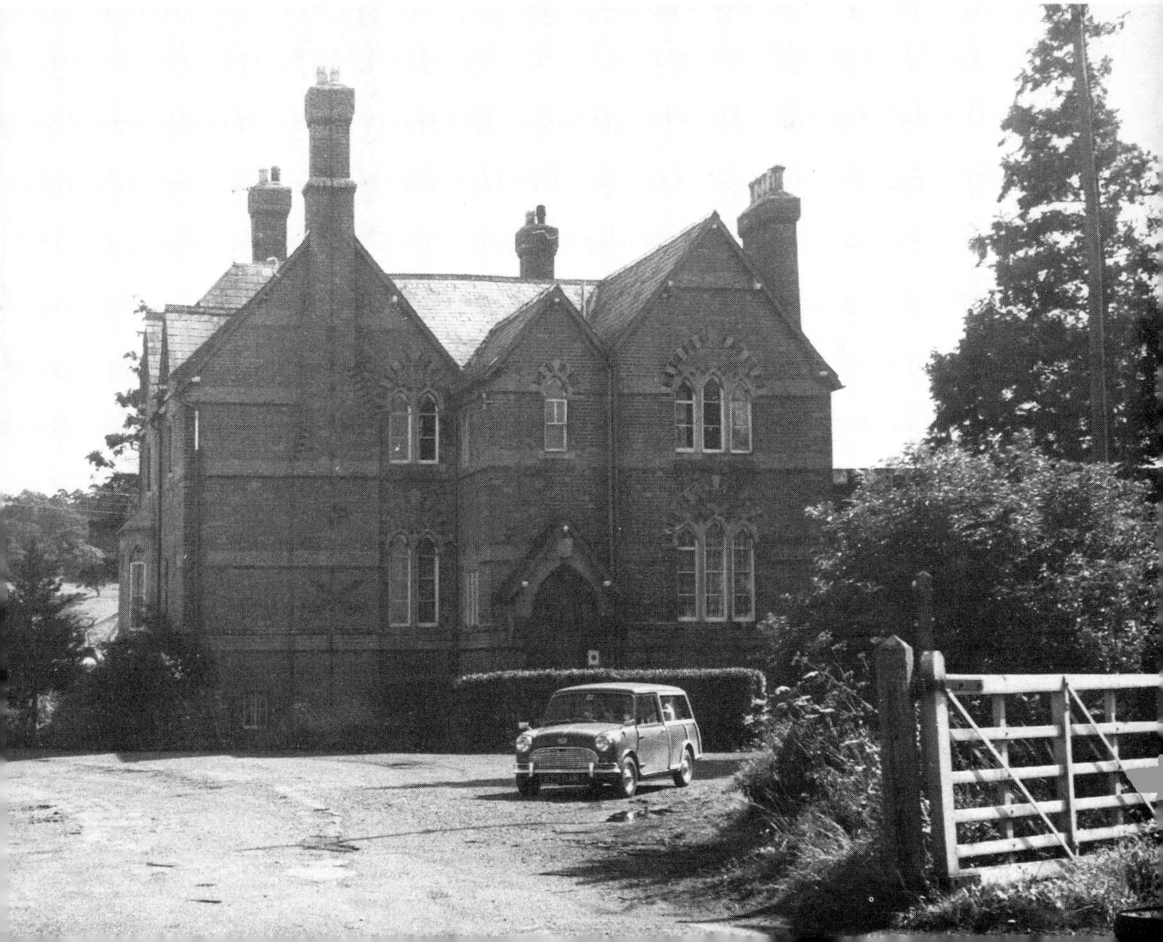

Wells Branch

Wells branch gradient profile. (C. Handley)

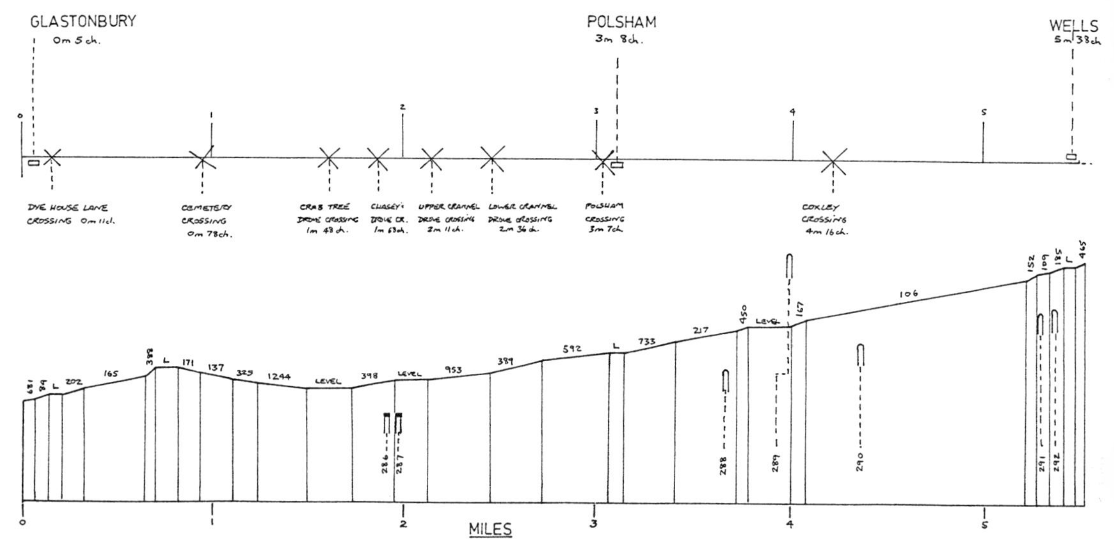

POLSHAM

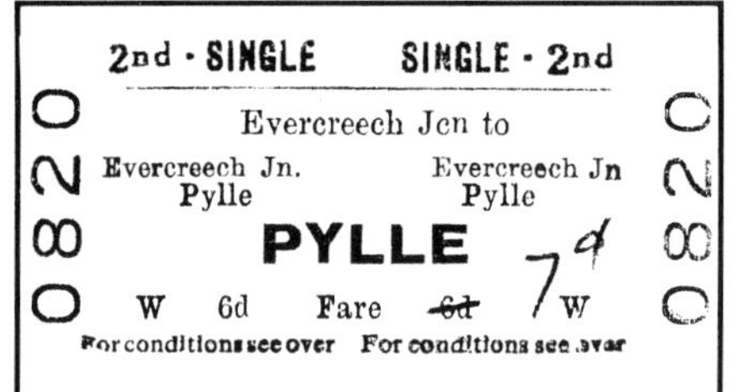

85. The only intermediate station on the branch, Polsham was opened in December 1861, mainly to serve the local agricultural community, as few people resided nearby. The oval disc seen on the ground frame hut was placed vertically or reverse side outwards if the service of the travelling signal lineman was required. As placed, it indicates "apparatus alright". (Private coll.)

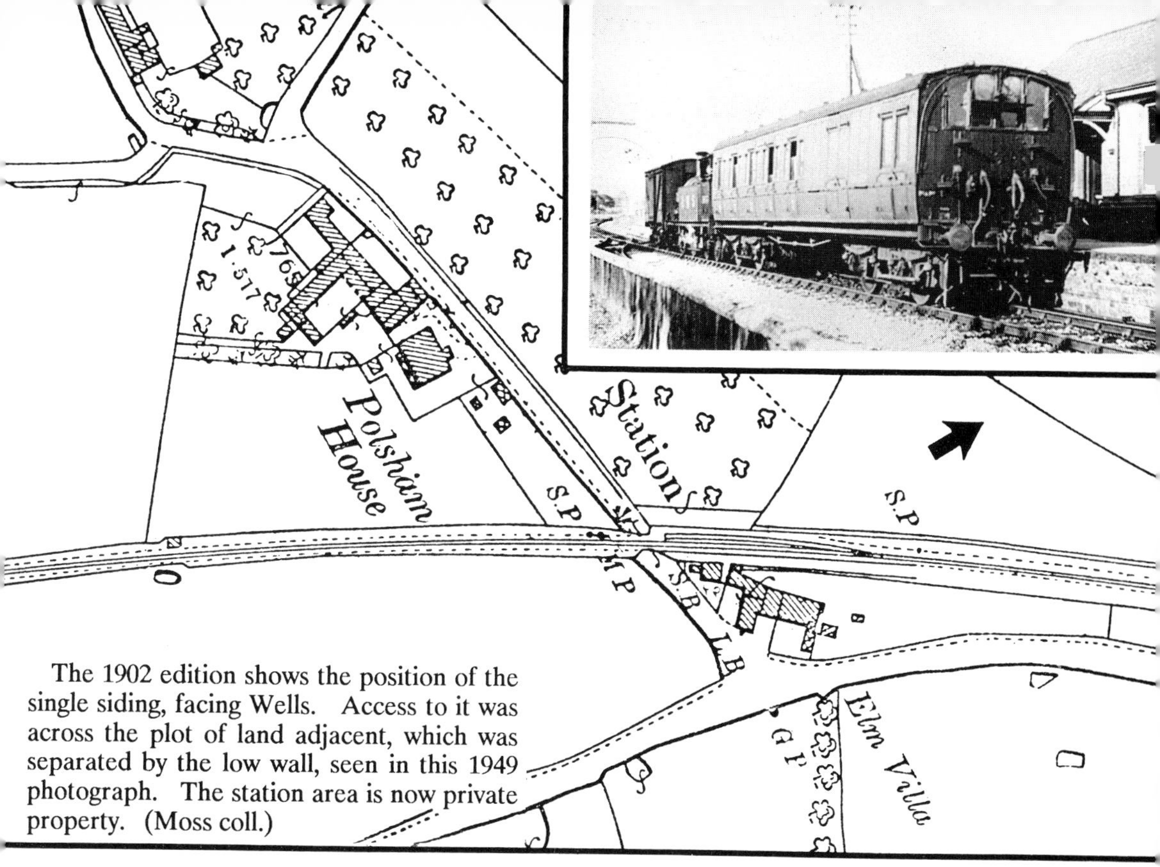

The 1902 edition shows the position of the single siding, facing Wells. Access to it was across the plot of land adjacent, which was separated by the low wall, seen in this 1949 photograph. The station area is now private property. (Moss coll.)

86. The slated building dated from 1894, the structures beyond it forming the original station. The house was added in the 1920s and a new rodding tunnel made under the platform ramp. The premises now form a fine home and the garden has been aptly adorned with a home signal, albeit GWR. This was the scene in 1949. (Moss coll.)

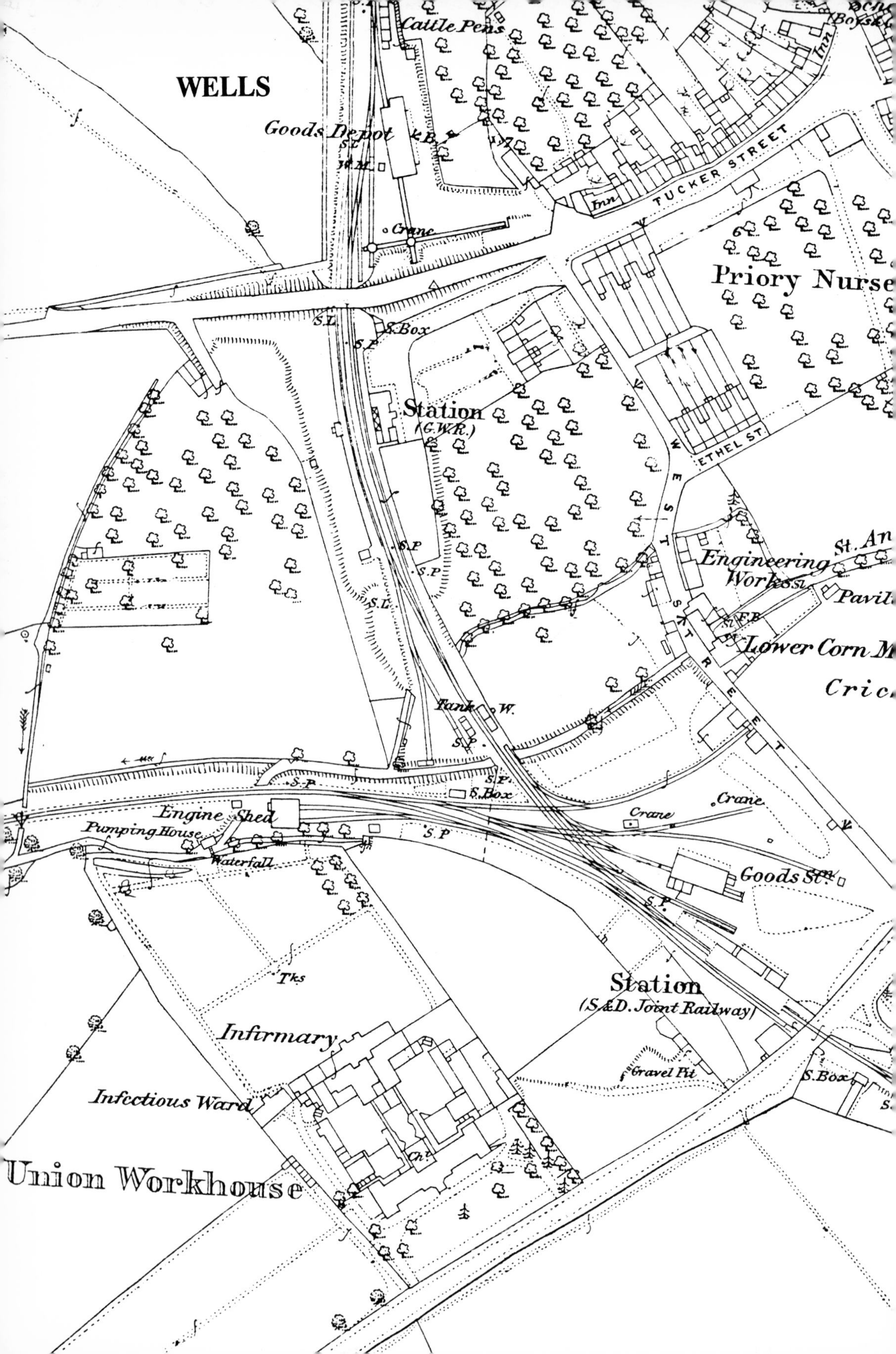

WELLS
Cattle Pens
Goods Depot
Crane
S.Box
Station
(G.W.R.)
Priory Nurse
TUCKER STREET
Inn
Inn
ETHEL ST.
WEST STREET
Engineering
Works
St. An
Pavil
Lower Corn M
Cric
Tank
S.Box
Engine Shed
Pumping House
Waterfall
Crane
Crane
Goods Stn
Station
(S.&D. Joint Railway)
Tks
Infirmary
Gravel Pit
S.Box
Infectious Ward
Chl
Union Workhouse

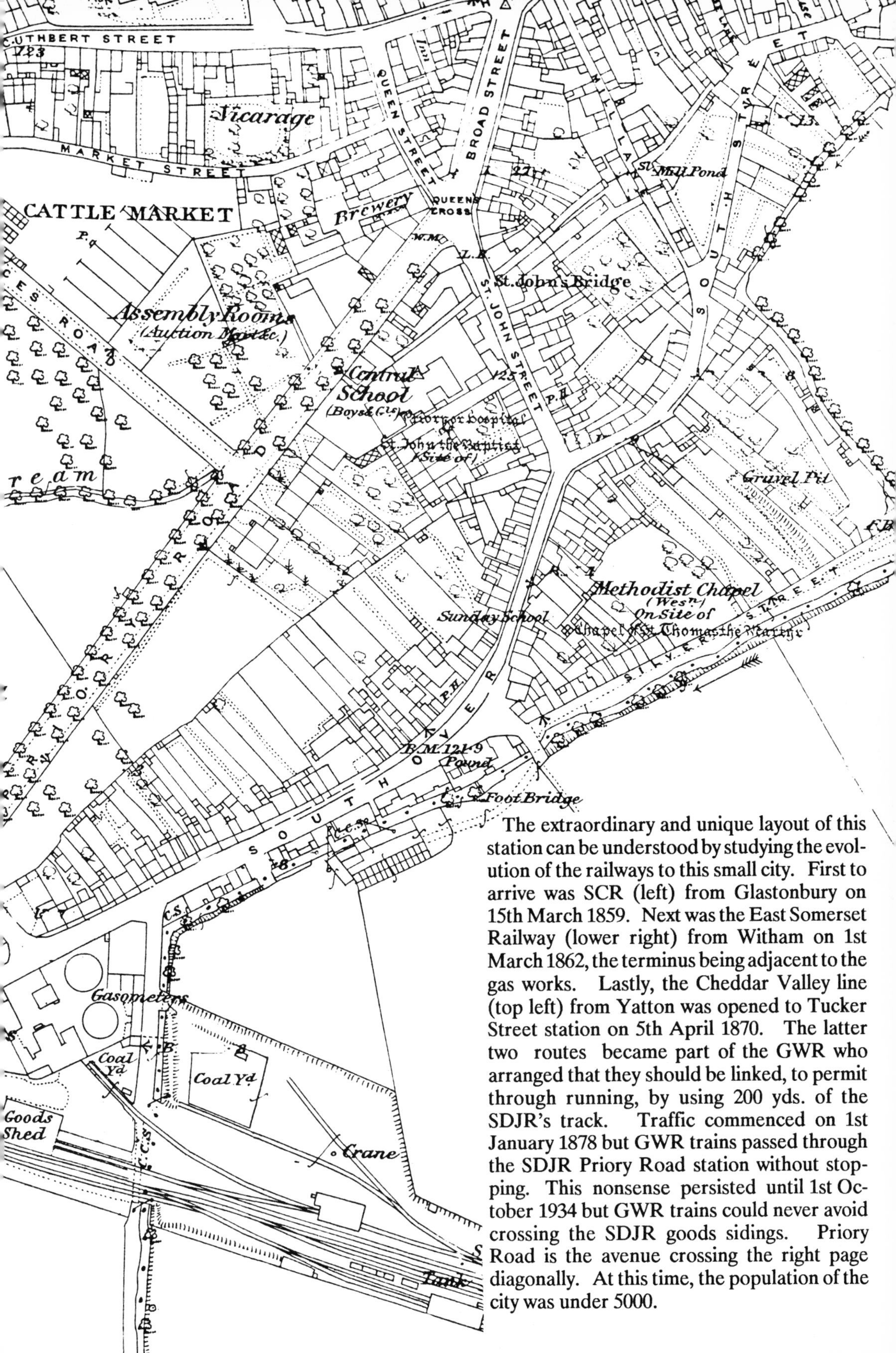

The extraordinary and unique layout of this station can be understood by studying the evolution of the railways to this small city. First to arrive was SCR (left) from Glastonbury on 15th March 1859. Next was the East Somerset Railway (lower right) from Witham on 1st March 1862, the terminus being adjacent to the gas works. Lastly, the Cheddar Valley line (top left) from Yatton was opened to Tucker Street station on 5th April 1870. The latter two routes became part of the GWR who arranged that they should be linked, to permit through running, by using 200 yds. of the SDJR's track. Traffic commenced on 1st January 1878 but GWR trains passed through the SDJR Priory Road station without stopping. This nonsense persisted until 1st October 1934 but GWR trains could never avoid crossing the SDJR goods sidings. Priory Road is the avenue crossing the right page diagonally. At this time, the population of the city was under 5000.

WELLS (PRIORY ROAD)

87. No. 54 departs for Glastonbury on 11th April 1914, the goods shed projecting above the rear coaches. The tracks in the foreground lead into the engine shed. The orientation can be clarified by reference to the map on the previous page. (K. Nunn/LCGB)

88. The camera was turned 180 degrees to reveal sister engine no. 55 in equally splendid condition standing outside its shed, which remained in use until 27th October 1951. It was demolished in December 1955. (K. Nunn/LCGB)

89. The overall roof complemented that at the SCR's other terminus but its design details and smoke hood were different. This is the view from the east end, looking towards the junction. (D. Cullum coll.)

A spring in the bishop's garden gave rise to the name and origin of Wells and the steady flow of fresh water passing the thresholds of the shops is a constant reminder of the importance of this divine gift. Most of the buildings of the city centre are of medieval origin but the greatest attraction to visitors is the beautiful cathedral with its 14th century clock and its highly ornate west facade, wider than it is tall. Products manufactured locally have included paper, brushes and cheese.

90. Mixed trains were worked regularly but this one was incomplete, as a brake van with tail lamp was required at the rear. The gradient of the connection to the GWR, beyond the level crossing, was 1 in 495 down towards the station, which required train crews to be particularly cautious.
(P. Rutherford/D. Cullum coll.)

91. The SDJR branch train (behind no. 1346) and signal box are seen in 1932 from the oil depot siding. The line to the GWR's Tucker Street station is visible between the two locomotives and the difficulty of shunting the SDJR goods yard is apparent. (Dr. I. C. Allen)

92. Upon arrival, the push-pull set prevented the passage of GWR trains, a problem during times of late running. Details of the driving compartment and a gas lamp on an old rail are notable. (D. Cullum coll.)

93. Two signal photographs from July 1949 show a rich variety. The bracket signals were of LSWR ancestry whereas the shunt signal was supplied by the SR for movements to the loop. The track layout changed several times during the life of the line. The water tank was filled from St. Andrew's Stream. (D. Cullum)

94. The view from East Somerset Box includes a GWR tapered wooden post, with co-acting arms, and a LSWR lattice post, which is fitted with sighting boards. Similar boards were in use at Salisbury, where GWR drivers were liable to overlook the delicate LSWR signals. The Esso Depot is on the left. (D. Cullum)

95. The west end in October 1951 displayed the name "Wells Priory Road" but the timetable still gave the distance to Tucker Street, as if Western Region trains did not stop at Priory Road. The suffix had been added in 1883. The signal design was known to some as "The Gallows". (S. C. Nash)

96. The 1.20pm mixed train departs on 2nd October 1951, earning no freight revenue and probably little from passengers as buses went to most popular destinations. The locomotive with the full BR lettering is no. 58046, formerly LMS no. 1298. (S. C. Nash)

97. Soon after cessation of passenger services on 29th October 1951, the roof was removed. The doors earlier led to the gentleman's toilet (unroofed section), the porter's room, waiting room and booking office. The tender of a BR locomotive is visible in the goods yard which remained in use until 13th July 1964.
(Lens of Sutton)

98. Only the platform, goods shed and crossing gates were to be seen in August 1968. The ex-GWR route lost its passenger service on 9th September 1963 and freight on 13th July 1964. In 1988, the goods shed was dismantled for re-erection on the East Somerset Railway, its wooden office going to the SDRT's premises at Washford on the West Somerset Railway. A new road now traverses the site.
(S. W. Baker)

WEST PENNARD

99. The cart contains milk churns and the coal wagon is marked "J. Snow & Co. Bristol". Two cattle wagons stand by the cattle pens, the "mucking-out" of which was amongst the duties of the station staff. (R. Shepherd)

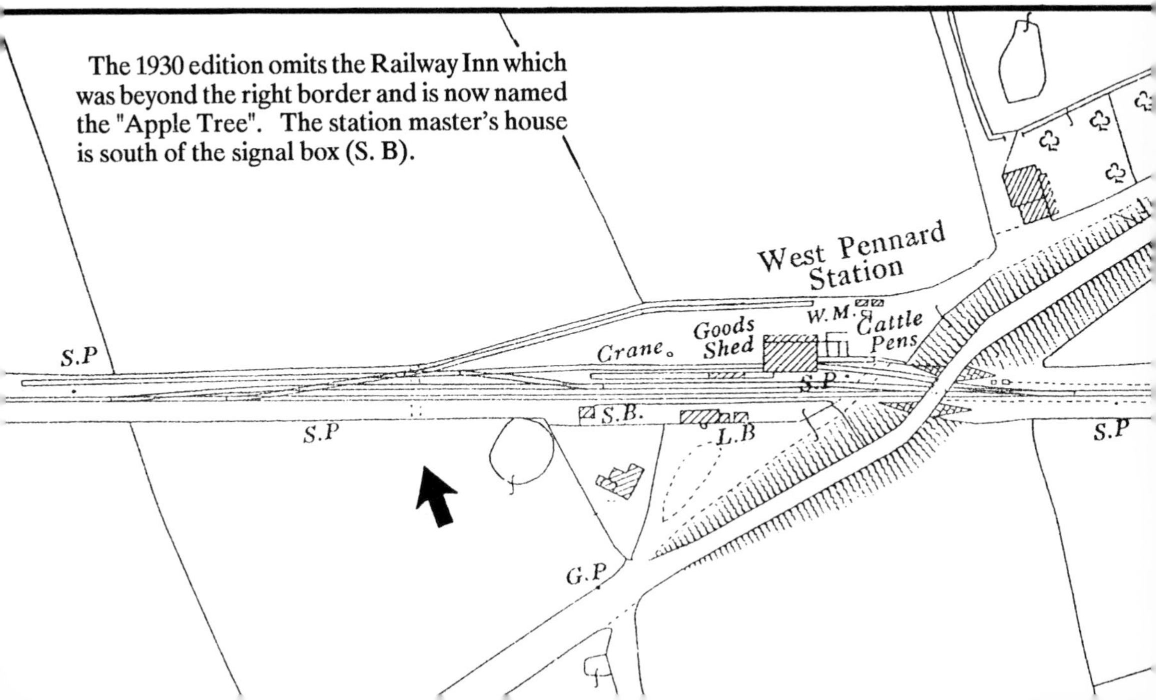

The 1930 edition omits the Railway Inn which was beyond the right border and is now named the "Apple Tree". The station master's house is south of the signal box (S. B).

RAC Gazetteer for 1936.

Pennard, West (P., 590). Pleasant spot, neighboured by woods. Noble Perp. hillside church (sloping floor, 16th-c. chancel-screen, tower, churchyard cross). Angling (apply stationmaster).

100. Many details reflect life on this typical country station - milk churns in profusion, a rambling rose on the signal box and signs of an antiseptic limewash on SDJR cattle wagon no. 12. Beyond the bridge the gradient can be seen to rise at 1 in 100 towards Pylle. (Lens of Sutton)

SOMERSET AND DORSET

101. No. 3201 (once SDJR no. 64) drifts down the gradient in 1934 and passes the hand cranked grindstone used by the track gangs for sharpening edge tools. The rear coaches are ex-MR and have clerestory roofs, the leading ones being of early 20th century SDJR origin. (Lens of Sutton)

← 102. The crossing gates were operated by hand but the large bolt visible was locked by lever no. 17 in the signal box. Seen departing east in 1958 is no. 43194, which started life as SDJR no. 62 in 1896. (C. L. Caddy)

103. The signal box had 23 levers and is seen in 1962 when it controlled the first passing loop on the branch. Staff regarded the Western Region locomotives as interlopers, this being one of the GWR's 2251 class. The station ceased to be manned on 25th June 1962. (C. L. Caddy)

BURNHAM-ON-SEA, BRIDGWATER, WELLS, GLASTONBURY AND STREET, and EVERCREECH JUNCTION—Somerset and Dorset—Southern & L M & S

Miles	Down.	Week Days only.							
		mrn		mrn		aft	aft	aft	aft
	Burnham-on-Sea...dep	9 45	..	1135	..	2 50	..	6 35	7 10
1½	Highbridge A 14, 20 arr	9 50	..	1140	..	2 55	..	6 40	7 15
	Highbridge dep	10 0	..	..	..	3 0	..	6 50	..
3½	Bason Bridge..............	10 4	..	..	..	3 4	..	6 55	..
6¾	Edington Junction..arr	1011	..	..	..	3 11	..	7 3	..
—	Edington Junc..dep	11 0	..	..	..	3 15	..	7 15	..
8½	Cossington........	11 5	..	..	..	3 20	..	7 20	..
11	Bawdrip Halt.....	1110	..	..	..	3 25	..	7 25	..
14	Bridgwater....arr	1122	..	..	..	3 37	..	7 37	..
—	Mls Bridgwater...dep	9 45	..	..	..	2 45	..	6 35	..
—	3 Bawdrip Halt.....	9 50	..	..	..	2 50	..	6 40	..
—	4¼ Cossington........	9 55	..	..	..	2 55	..	6 45	..
—	7¼ Edington Junc..arr	10 7	..	..	..	3 7	..	6 57	..
—	Edington Junction..dep	1012	..	..	..	3 12	..	7 5	..
9	Shapwick J..............	1018	..	..	..	3 18	..	7 11	..
11	Ashcott K..............	1022	..	..	..	3 22	..	7 15	..
13½	Glastonbury & Street arr	1030	..	..	..	3 30	..	7 24	..
—	Glastonbury G dep	1040	..	..	..	..	6 20	7 35	..
16¾	Polsham Halt.....	1045	..	..	..	..	6 25	7 40	..
19½	Wells L ......arr	1057	..	..	..	..	6 37	7 53	..
—	Mls Wells L ......dep	1010	..	..	..	3 10	..	7 5	..
—	2½ Polsham Halt.....	1015	..	..	..	3 15	..	7 10	..
—	5½ Glastonbury G arr	1026	..	..	..	3 26	..	7 21	..
—	Glastonbury & Street dep	1035	..	..	..	3 33	..	7 33	..
19	West Pennard..........	1045	..	..	..	3 44	..	7 45	..
22½	Pylle..................	1053	..	..	..	3 50	..	7 53	..
24	Evercreech Junc. C arr	11 0	..	..	..	3 58	..	8 0	..

Up.	Week Days only.								
	mrn	mrn		aft	aft	aft	aft	aft	aft
Evercreech Junc....dep	..	10 5	..	1 0	..	..	550	..	9 25
Pylle..................	..	1010	..	1 5	..	..	555	..	..
West Pennard..........	..	1017	..	1 12	..	..	6 2	..	9 36
Glastonbury & Street arr	..	1026	..	1 23	..	..	612	..	9 47
Glastonbury G dep	..	1040	..	1 30	..	..	620	..	..
Polsham Halt.....	..	1045	..	1 35	..	..	625	..	..
Wells L.......arr	..	1057	..	1 47	..	..	637	..	..
Wells L.......dep	..	1010	..	1 5	..	310	..	7 5	..
Polsham Halt.....	..	1015	..	1 10	..	315	..	7 10	..
Glastonbury G arr	..	1026	..	1 21	..	326	..	7 21	..
Glastonbury & Street dep	8 15	1035	..	1 28	..	Stp	615	Stop	9 50
Ashcott K..............	8 21	1045	..	1 35	..		623		..
Shapwick J..............	8 28	1050	..	1 41	..	..	629	..	..
Edington Junction.. arr	8 36	1057	..	1 47	..	..	636	..	10 7
Edington Junc..dep	8 50	11 0	..	1 50	..	..	715	..	..
Cossington........	8 55	11 5	..	1 55	..	..	720	..	..
Bawdrip Halt....	9 0	1110	..	2 6	..	..	725	..	..
Bridgwater ..arr	9 12	1122	..	2 12	..	..	737	aft	..
Bridgwater...dep	Stop	9 45	..	1 20	245	..	..	6 35	..
Bawdrip Halt.....		9 50	..	1 25	250	..	..	6 40	..
Cossington........	..	9 55	..	1 30	255	..	..	6 45	..
Edington Junc..arr	..	10 7	..	1 42	3 7	..	..	6 57	..
Edington Junction..dep	..	1058	..	1 48	..	..	637	..	10 8
Bason Bridge..........	..	11 5	..	1 58	..	..	644	..	..
Highbridge A 14, 20 arr	mrn	1111	..	2 4	..	aft	650	..	1020
Highbridge dep	9 30	1120	..	2 15	..	615	655	..	..
Burnham-on-Sea. arr	9 35	1125	..	2 20	..	620	7 0	..	..

A Adjoining G.W. Sta. C Station for Castle Cary (3 miles) G Glastonbury and Street.
J Station for Westhay (1 mile). K Station for Meare (1¼ miles). L Priory Road. m Third class only.

1944

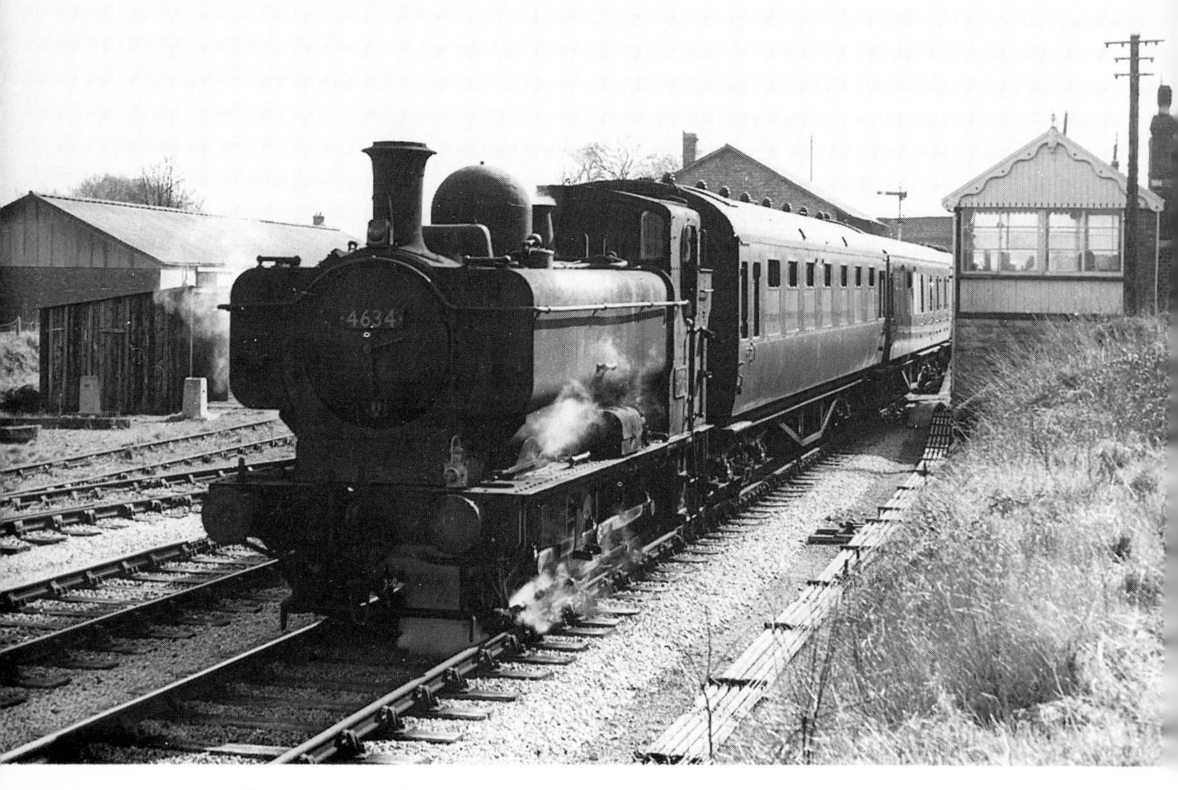

104. Another ex-GWR locomotive to work the branch was 5700 class 0-6-0PT no. 4634, seen passing the hut for the permanent way trolley. The large building behind it was erected in WWII as a government store and gave rise to some rail traffic. The goods yard closed on 10th June 1963. (C. L. Caddy)

106. Looking over the bridge in 1968, we see the 7-ton hand worked crane and the name-board still standing. The route was perfectly straight from here, across Splotts Moor to the A30 overbridge, north of Glastonbury, a distance of three and a half miles. The main buildings were still standing, over twenty years later. (S. W. Baker)

So. West. and Mid. Railway Companies'

Som. and Dor. Joint Line.

TO

EDINGTON JUNCTION.

105. The signal box was closed on 26th August 1964 and the loop taken out of use. This is the scene in February 1966, a month before closure. The now demolished bridge carried the A361, the village being over a mile to the south-west. (S. W. Baker)

107. Half a mile east of West Pennard w
Steam Bow Crossing, one of nine on the branc
provided with staff cottages. (D. Milton)

Level crossings with cottages

Name	Location
Huntspill	Bason Bridge - Edington Junction
Catcott	Edington Junction - Shapwick
Sharpham	Ashcott - Glastonbury
Aqueduct	Ditto
Cemetery Lane	Glastonbury - West Pennard
Pennard Lane	Ditto
Steam Bow	West Pennard - Pylle
Cock Mill	Ditto
Elbow Corner	Pylle - Evercreech Junction

The list above was compiled from the WWII control diagram. The crossings on the branches are shown with the appropriate gradient profile.

→

109. The line passed over Cock Mill Crossi
before reaching the station, which was 225
above sea level and nearly at the summit of t
route. The crossover at the end of the pl
form was removed in May 1960 but the remai
ing siding was usable until 26th June 19
(Lens of Sutton)

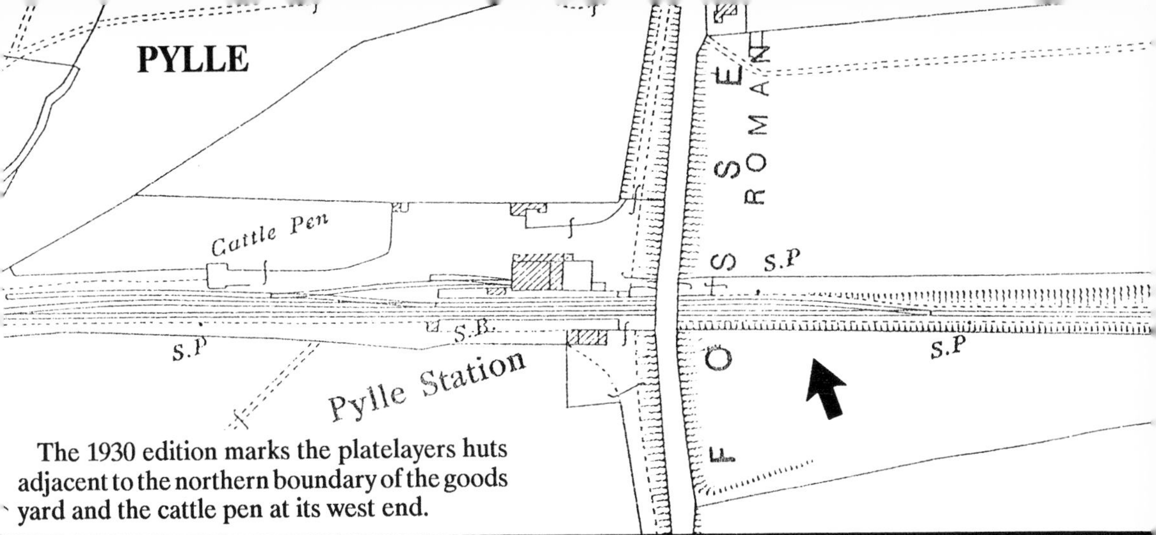

The 1930 edition marks the platelayers huts adjacent to the northern boundary of the goods yard and the cattle pen at its west end.

108. Opened with the line, Pylle (pronounced "pill") lost its passing loop in 1929 and its staff in 1957. This August 1956 photograph includes the 17-lever box which had acted simply as a ground frame since 1929. Home and distant signals in each direction were retained. (R. M. Casserley)

110. No. 41248 makes its obligatory stop with the 5.10pm from Highbridge on 17th July 1960. The paved area in the right foreground was once the milk dock. In the distance was a limestone quarry which was given rail access in 1869 when a private siding was laid to serve *THE PYLLE LIME KILN COMPANY*, which was known locally as "Pylle Limeworks". The siding was controlled by a ground frame worked by a tablet from Pylle signal-box and a disc and crossbar signal remained in use here for many years. Late in 1905 the company, now producing both lime and cement, was the subject of a take-over becoming *FARRANCE & BOYTON LTD. LIME & CEMENT WORKS*, but by the end of 1912 the siding was closed. (T. Wright)

111. This 1963 photograph records the unusual attached station master's house and goods shed. In 1989, the former was used as a dwelling and the latter for packing meat, having been extended across the trackbed. The station has been tastefully extended for residential purposes. (C. L. Caddy)

112. Pylle (Halt), as the nameboard declares, was one mile from the village which recorded 260 inhabitants in 1877 and 200 in 1901. John Betjeman, poet laureate to-be, soliloquized in 1963 - "I doubt if there's a quieter, sadder sight in Somerset than Pylle, when the train has left and it sinks back to silence". (Lens of Sutton)

113. Elbow Corner Crossing was on the approach to Evercreech Junction, on the south side of the line. The elbow referred to the alignment of the road. The cottage and gates still existed in 1988. (Pamlin Prints)

EVERCREECH JUNCTION

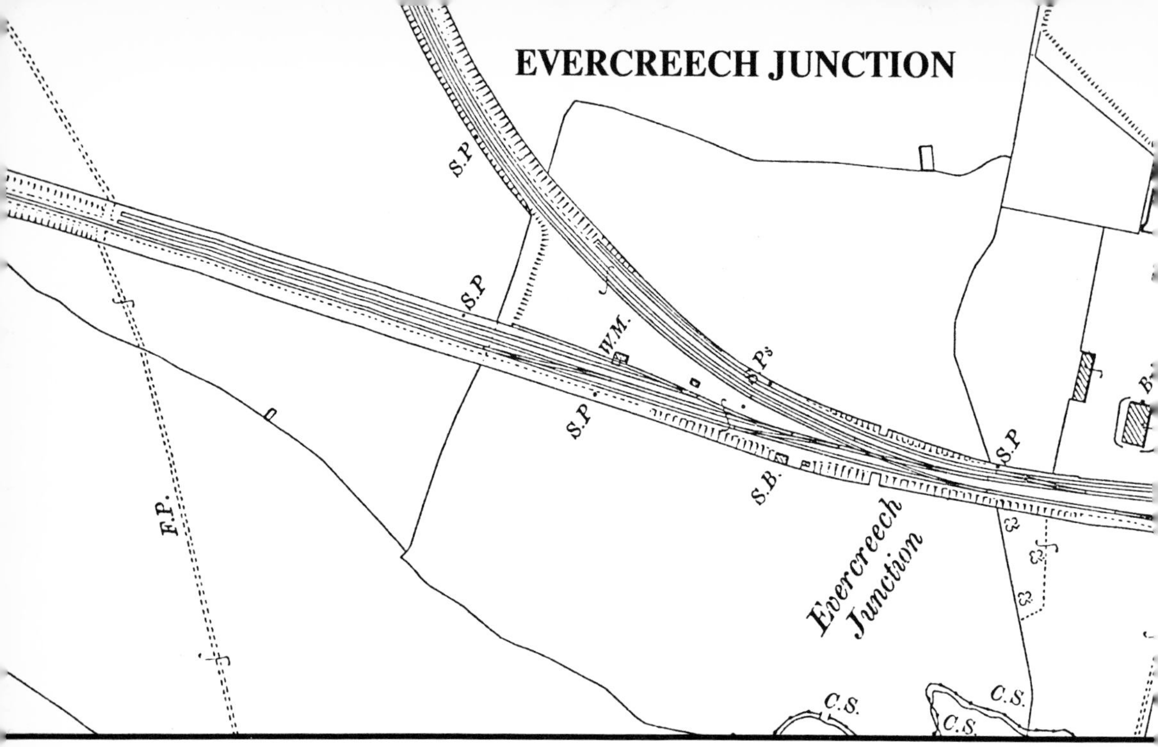

114. Near the western end of the half mile long site was Evercreech North Box which had 32 levers to control the junction and approaches to the yards. The single line token is being offered to the crew of class 2 no. 41296, as it leaves for Highbridge on 22nd July 1958. (R. C. Riley)

Bradshaw listed the station as "Evercreech for Ditcheat" until it became a junction with the opening of the Bath line on 20th July 1874. This map is the 1901 revision, reproduced at 20" to 1 mile, to show the full extent of the sidings. This makes an interesting comparison with the 1st edition of 1884, reproduced below pictures 111 and 112 in our *Bournemouth to Evercreech Junction* and sadly supplied to us wrongly dated. The later developments, which included provision of a turntable and additional sidings, are shown in a diagram below pictures 115 and 116 in our *Bath to Evercreech Junction* volume. The short siding to the left of the cattle sale yard was used by the slaughter house.

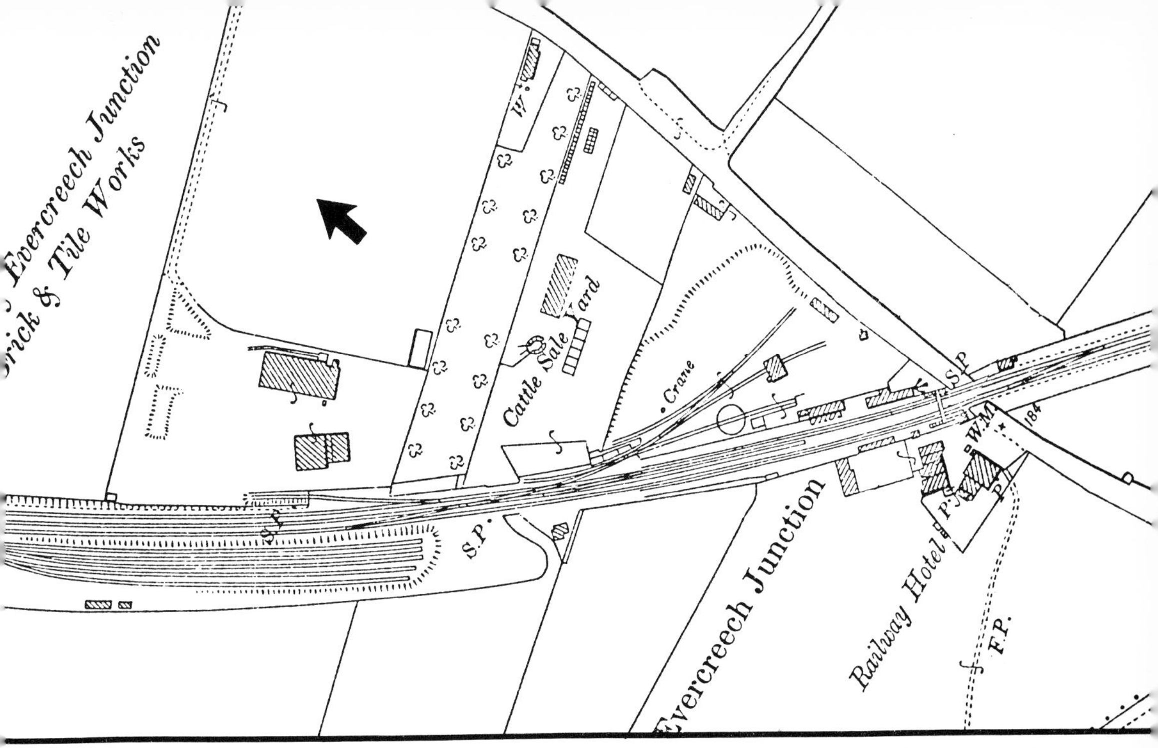

115. Behind North Box is the shunting neck to the marshalling yard, which was in use 24 hours a day, until through freight services were withdrawn. The line to the left of the spare sleepers led to the turntable, which was of 56 ft length and had been installed in about 1934. It replaced a 50 ft one which had been supplied by the LSWR around 30 years earlier. We witness the departure of 0-6-0 no. 44272 with the 9.55am on 18th May 1963.
(C. L. Caddy)

PASSENGERS MUST CROSS THE LINE
BY THE FOOT BRIDGE

116. South Box worked the gates by means of a wheel, which had extended spokes, as on the bridge of a ship. The footbridge by the ivy clad station house was used by countless passengers changing to and from the branch to Burnham. (Lens of Sutton)

117. The middle road was used by banking engines or, as here, Highbridge branch trains awaiting arrival of up trains. On the left of this March 1962 panorama is the shunting bell and telephone with which the shunter communicates with South Box, which is visible beyond the footbridge. Also on the left is the local goods yard and shed which remained open longer than most, closing on 29th November 1965. It had two cranes, one of seven tons capacity and the other rated at one ton. (E. Wilmshurst)

118. No. 43248 stands outside the station master's house, which overshadowed the small station buildings, all of which still exist. The train was the 4.0pm from Highbridge on 19th July 1958, arriving at 5.0pm and giving a 20 minute connection into the Manchester train, which reached Bournemouth West at 7.23pm. (S. W. Baker)

←

119. A single coach sufficed for the 9.55am service to Highbridge on 29th May 1965, when no. 41307 was sadly caked with grime. It was probably also not in perfect mechanical condition, not essential on the branch with its 40 mph speed limit. (C. L. Caddy)

120. The same train is seen departing past the marshalling sidings which were level, the main line being on a 1 in 105 gradient. The junction frustrated many waiting passengers in its early years, delighted numerous steam enthusiasts in the 1950s and saddened all when it closed on 6th March 1966. (C. L. Caddy)

Miles	Down		Week Days only				
			a.m	A a.m	A p.m	p.m	p.m
—	Highbridge and Burnham-on-Sea	dep	7 0	9 50	2 20	4 15	7 5
1½	Bason Bridge	"	7 4	9 54	2 24	4 19	7 9
5	Edington Burtle	"	7 12	10 3	2 33	4 28	7 20
7¼	Shapwick L	"	7 18	10 9	2 39	4 34	7 26
9¼	Ashcott M	"	7 23	1014	2 44	4 39	7 31
12	Glastonbury and Street	"	7 33	1023	2 53	4 48	7 43
17¼	West Pennard	"	7 44	1034	3 4	5 0	7 54
20¾	Pylle	"	7 54	1044	3 14	5 12	8 4
22¼	Evercreech Junc. W	arr	8 0	1050	3 20	5 18	8 10

Miles	Up		Week Days only						
			a.m	a.m	SX p.m	SO p.m	p.m	p.m	p.m
—	Evercreech Junc. W	dep	8 20	9 55	1 15	1 20	4 48	6 2	9 30
1½	Pylle	"	8 25	10 0	1 20	1 25	4 53	6 7	D
5	West Pennard	"	8 33	10 8	1 28	1 33	5 1	6 15	9 40
10¼	Glastonbury and Street	"	8 45	1025	1 40	1 45	5 13	6 30	9 52
13	Ashcott M	"	8 52	1033	1 48	1 52	5 21	6 38	D
15	Shapwick L	"	8 57	1040	1 53	1 58	5 26	6 43	D
17¼	Edington Burtle	"	9 3	1047	2 0	2 4	5 33	6 49	1010
21	Bason Bridge	"	9 11	1055	2 8	2 13	5 41	6 58	D
22¼	Highbridge and Burnham-on-Sea	arr	9 16	11 0	2 13	2 18	5 46	7 4	1020

A Through Train to Templecombe
D Stops to set down passengers if required, Guard to be informed

L Station for Westhay (1 mile)
M Station for Meare (1¼ miles)

SO Saturdays only
SX Saturdays excepted
W Station for Castle Cary (3 miles)

1954

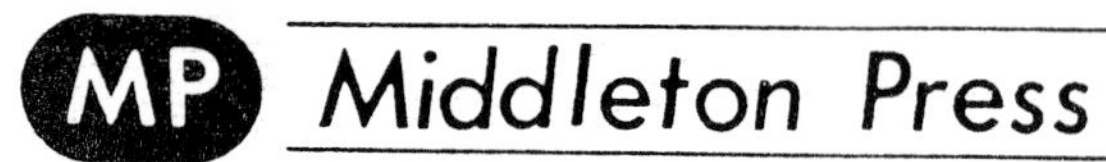

Easebourne Lane, Midhurst. West Sussex. GU29 9AZ
(0730) 813169

BRANCH LINES

BRANCH LINES TO MIDURST
BRANCH LINES AROUND MIDHURST
BRANCH LINES TO HORSHAM
BRANCH LINES TO ALTON
BRANCH LINE TO HAYLING
BRANCH LINE TO SOUTHWOLD
BRANCH LINE TO TENTERDEN
BRANCH LINES TO NEWPORT
BRANCH LINES TO TUNBRIDGE WELLS
BRANCH LINE TO SWANAGE
BRANCH LINES TO LONGMOOR
BRANCH LINE TO LYME REGIS
BRANCH LINE TO FAIRFORD
BRANCH LINE TO ALLHALLOWS
BRANCH LINES AROUND ASCOT
BRANCH LINES AROUND WEYMOUTH
BRANCH LINE TO HAWKHURST

SOUTH COAST RAILWAYS

BRIGHTON TO WORTHING
CHICHESTER TO PORTSMOUTH
BRIGHTON TO EASTBOURNE
RYDE TO VENTNOR
EASTBOURNE TO HASTINGS
PORTSMOUTH TO SOUTHAMPTON
SOUTHAMPTON TO BOURNEMOUTH
ASHFORD TO DOVER
BOURNEMOUTH TO WEYMOUTH

SOUTHERN MAIN LINES

WOKING TO PORTSMOUTH
HAYWARDS HEATH TO SEAFORD
EPSOM TO HORSHAM
CRAWLEY TO LITTLEHAMPTON
THREE BRIDGES TO BRIGHTON
WATERLOO TO WOKING
VICTORIA TO EAST CROYDON
TONBRIDGE TO HASTINGS
EAST CROYDON TO THREE BRIDGES
WOKING TO SOUTHAMPTON
WATERLOO TO WINDSOR
LONDON BRIDGE TO EAST CROYDON

COUNTRY RAILWAY ROUTES

BOURNEMOUTH TO EVERCREECH JNCT
READING TO GUILDFORD
WOKING TO ALTON
BATH TO EVERCREECH JUNCTION
GUILDFORD TO REDHILL
EAST KENT LIGHT RAILWAY
FAREHAM TO SALISBURY
BURNHAM TO EVERCREECH JUNCTION

STEAMING THROUGH

STEAMING THROUGH KENT
STEAMING THROUGH EAST HANTS
STEAMING THROUGH SURREY
STEAMING THROUGH WEST SUSSEX
STEAMING THROUGH THE ISLE OF WIGHT
STEAMING THROUGH WEST HANTS

OTHER RAILWAY BOOKS

WAR ON THE LINE
GARRAWAY FATHER & SON
LONDON CHATHAM & DOVER RAILWAY
INDUSTRIAL RAILWAYS OF THE SOUTH EAST

OTHER BOOKS

MIDHURST TOWN THEN & NOW
EAST GRINSTEAD THEN & NOW

MILITARY DEFENCE OF WEST SUSSEX
SUSSEX POLICE FORCES

WEST SUSSEX WATERWAYS
SURREY WATERWAYS
KENT AND EAST SUSSEX WATERWAYS